Remembering the Power of Words

WOMEN AND POLITICS IN THE PACIFIC NORTHWEST
Series editor: Dr. Melody Rose, Portland State University

This series explores the many roles women have played in Northwest politics, both historically and in modern times. Taking a broad definition of political activity, the series examines the role of women in elected office and the barriers to their role in the electoral arena, as well as the examples of women as advocates and agitators outside the halls of power. Illuminating the various roles played by diverse and under-represented groups of women and considering the differences among and between groups of women, acknowledging that women of the Northwest do not experience politics in a single, uniform way, are particular goals of this series.

The photograph on the previous page shows Avel holding a photo of the members of the N.A.A.C.P. Portland Branch who lobbied for passage of Oregon's Public Accommodations Act in 1953 and the legislators who sponsored it. This historical photograph how hangs at Senator Gordly's initiative outside the Oregon House of Representatives chamber as a memorial to that historic achievement. Photograph by Charles Waugh, Charles Fine Art Portraits.

Remembering the Power of Words

THE LIFE OF AN OREGON ACTIVIST, LEGISLATOR, AND COMMUNITY LEADER

by

Avel Louise Gordly
with
Patricia A. Schechter

OREGON STATE UNIVERSITY PRESS

CORVALLIS

The paper in this book meets the guidelines for permanence and durability of the Committee on Production Guidelines for Book Longevity of the Council on Library Resources and the minimum requirements of the American National Standard for Permanence of Paper for Printed Library Materials Z39.48-1984.

Library of Congress Cataloging-in-Publication Data
Gordly, Avel Louise, 1947-
  Remembering the power of words : the life of an Oregon activist, legislator, and community leader / by Avel Louise Gordly with Patricia A. Schechter.
       p. cm. -- (Women and politics in the Pacific Northwest)
  Includes bibliographical references and index.
  ISBN 978-0-87071-604-1 (alk. paper)
  1. Gordly, Avel Louise, 1947- 2. African American politicians--Oregon--Biography. 3. Women politicians--Oregon--Biography. 4. African American women--Oregon--Biography. 5. Community activists--Oregon--Biography. 6. Oregon--Politics and government--1951- I. Schechter, Patricia Ann, 1964- II. Title.
  F881.35.G67A3 2011
  324.2092--dc22
  [B]
                                                                2010049231

Oregon State University Press
121 The Valley Library
Corvallis OR 97331-4501
541-737-3166 • fax 541-737-3170
http://oregonstate.edu/dept/press

DEDICATION

To
my parents, Beatrice Bernice Coleman Gordly and Fay Lee Gordly
my grandmothers, Lessie Gordly and Alberta Louise Randolph
and
my courageous son Tyrone Wayne Waters

I prefer to be true to myself, even at the hazard of incurring the ridicule of others, rather than to be false, and to incur my own abhorrence.—Frederick Douglass

While we wait in silence for that final luxury of fearlessness, the weight of that silence will choke us.—Audre Lorde

Successful leadership depends on a fundamental shift of being, including a deep committment to the dream and a passion for serving versus being driven by the pursuit of status and power
—Joseph Jaworksi, founder, American Leadership Forum

For God hath not given us the spirit of fear, but of power, and of a sound mind.—2 Timothy 1:7 *KJV*

TABLE OF CONTENTS

A list of bills introduced by Avel Gordly as a state legislator can be found at http://hdl.handle.net/1957/19543

Foreword

I have known Avel Gordly since we were third graders in a Portland
public school. That would have been about 1955-56, shortly after
passage of Oregon's Public Accommodations Act in 1953. The first
page of this memoir shows Avel holding a photo of the members
of the N.A.A.C.P. Portland Branch who lobbied for that Act and the
legislators who sponsored it on the day the Act was passed. Members
of the N.A.A.C.P. lobbied for eighteen legislative sessions—that's
thirty-six years—before they succeeded in having a law passed that
prohibited discrimination in public accommodations. Prior to the Act,
African Americans were prohibited from most restaurants, hotels,
swimming pools, amusement parks, and even hospitals. My parents
Otto and Verdell Rutherford were leading the organization at the
time the Act was passed and they are in the picture. I am honored
that Avel has paid tribute to my parents and their comrades for their
volunteer service and that she has asked me to write this foreword.

It is fitting that Avel has chosen to include this picture for a
couple of reasons. First, the picture conveys Avel's feeling that she
is standing on the shoulders of those who came before her and that
she has carried the legacy of those early activists forward in her roles
as activist, legislator, and educator.

Second, the picture shows the results of a collaborative effort.
This memoir is also the result of collaboration between Avel and
Patricia Schechter, her friend and colleague from Portland State
University. Patricia interviewed Avel as a participant in an oral history
project. The interview has evolved into this book—an opportunity
for the reader to see the private face behind a public person.

Avel's public life is a matter of public record. For a complete
professional biography, see http://www.pdx.edu/blackstudies/
avel-gordly-biography. Briefly stated, Avel served in the Oregon
State Legislature from 1991 to 2008. After serving three terms as

a member of the House of Representatives, Avel was elected as Oregon's first female African American State Senator in 1996. She retired from that position in 2008.

In addition to serving on various task forces and committees, during her tenure in office Avel was the chief petitioner for a constitutional amendment that removed racist language from the Oregon Constitution and for Oregon's minimum wage law. She also sponsored the Expanded Options Bill, which many educators and advocates believed was the singular educational achievement of the 2005 legislative session; the Oregon Legislative Assembly's Day of Acknowledgment, renouncing Oregon's legacy of institutional racism; and the first legislation in the nation to address the issue of children abducted by family members or others into whose care the children had been entrusted.

Among other legislation she sponsored were bills:

— proclaiming Juneteenth, June 19 of each year, the day on which slavery was abolished in Texas in 1865, as a day for celebration statewide of dignity and freedom of all citizens;

— creating the Governor's Environmental Justice Task Force, which requires state agencies and the governor to work on issues of environmental justice in Oregon;

—requiring every county police force to be trained in the use of appropriate deadly force;

—creating the statewide Office of Multicultural Health;

—requiring the availability of health care interpreters and the inclusion of people of diverse backgrounds on state health licensing boards.

Avel introduced resolutions honoring the lives, achievements, and heroism of Oregon citizens, including my parents, McKinley Burt, Bill McClendon, Ruth Ascher, Hon. Roosevelt Robinson, and Hon. Mercedes Deiz. Moreover, she organized a ceremony marking the fiftieth anniversary of the passage of the Public Accommodations Act, and honoring U.S. Senator Mark Hatfield, who carried the bill to passage as a young state legislator and is among those pictured in the photograph on the first page.

She also served on the Public Commission on the Legislature (appointed by Senate President) and the Mental Health Alignment Work group (appointed by Governor Kitzhaber).

Avel's personal story is one of faith and perseverance in the face of adversity, while dealing with clinical depression. Anyone who has battled depression while holding down a responsible position will identify with Avel's observations. Anyone who is faced with doubts about whether he or she is up to the challenge of single parenting or any single parent who wants more from life will gain strength from her story. Anyone who believes that social change is possible and that individuals can accomplish it will be encouraged by Avel's story. It is a story of self-creation, preparation, and taking advantage of opportunities when they presented themselves, even when faced with self-doubt. Avel has lived a life of service and she has blazed a trail of Black female "firsts." Her story includes her personal challenges and growth and how that growth has affected and improved the communities she has served. I urge teachers to use this book as an example of a local role model for youngsters.

Let me set the historical context for Avel's story. In 1940, there were fewer than two thousand African Americans in Portland (0.06 percent of the population). By 1950, the percentage had increased to 2.5 percent, still fewer than ten thousand African Americans in a total population of 374,000. Black people have always been true "minorities" in Portland. When Avel and I were young children, there were few Black professionals in Portland and job opportunities for Black people were mostly limited to service jobs.

Avel and I were both born in 1947 and grew up during a time of great change. We are old enough to remember "Old Portland" with its vibrant, mostly segregated Black community, largely situated near where the Coliseum now stands and with Black-owned businesses along Williams Avenue. (Avel and her siblings still own the family home on N. Williams Ave. and have succeeded thus far in avoiding the forces of gentrification.) We also remember having to sit in the balcony at segregated movie theaters and being able to skate at the segregated roller rink on only one night a week. We were raised at a time when mothers stayed at home, or if they worked, most were domestics for white families because there were few jobs; and patriarchy was the norm.

Avel and I both come from traditional two-parent working-class families. Both of our fathers had worked for the railroad at one time and lived in Oregon at a time when the state constitution said "Negroes" could not be in the state. They actively fought against the discrimination and exclusion faced by African Americans. Our parents had high expectations of us and we had high expectations for ourselves. Our parents were our role models. We believed that everything we did reflected on our family and our race and we were obliged to do our best and not embarrass either.

By the time of our teens and early twenties, because of local and nationwide agitation and struggle that led to new laws, both African Americans and women had found their voices and America was forever changed. Even though there was much work yet to be done, new opportunities were being created. Being both Black and female, we were affected by both movements and our lives are the result of those times.

I always felt that I was under the microscope of the Black community when I was growing up. Most Black people knew each other and I was "Otto and Verdell's girl." I felt it was a burden to be the daughter of two people who were so well known. I just wanted to be "Charlotte," so I kept leaving Portland, moving to Los Angeles right out of high school and eventually ending up at Howard University School of Law in Washington, D.C., during the unpleasant Reagan era.

After finishing law school, I worked as a civil rights attorney for the N.A.A.C.P. Legal Defense and Educational Fund, Inc., in D.C. and New York City during a time when the courts were overturning much of the progress that had been made in the 1970s. It became clear to me that using traditional civil rights laws and the courts to expand opportunities to gain equity for African Americans had reached its end. I returned to Oregon to assist my elderly parents and worked in the public sector as an administrative law judge until recently retiring.

Avel and I worked together in community organizations before I left for law school. During the period that I was away from Portland, Avel was elected to the state legislature. That role put her in a strong public light. I have watched in awe as Avel has opened her life to the public and made sometimes unpopular decisions based on her convictions and integrity—which is not the way the legislative game is usually played. She maintained her focus and was not swayed by the moneyed interests. She has sponsored meaningful legislation and ensured that the State of Oregon recognized Black Oregonians' contributions. And now that she has retired from the senate, she is continuing to serve the community by passing on her knowledge and insights to students at Portland State University.

Avel and I came of age at a time when things were improving for African Americans and for women. We were fortunate enough to be informed and influenced by the struggles of our parents to believe that we could make a difference and that we were obliged to try to do so regardless of the personal obstacles we may have faced. This book should be required reading for all who are interested in the history of Oregon's diverse public servants. Senator Avel Gordly has certainly been of great service to Oregonians in general, and African American Oregonians, in particular. She is deserving of accolades and tributes in honor of that service. I am proud and thankful that I can call her my sisterfriend.

Charlotte B. Rutherford
Portland, Oregon
August 15, 2010

Acknowledgements

Gratitude. A wonderful word that captures all that I am feeling at this moment in my God-blessed life. As I acknowledge everyone who helped and supported the writing of this memoir, gratefulness kept coming to my heart and mind. Thank you to one who has become a dear sisterfriend, Patricia Schechter, for the love, inspiration, trust, mentoring, laughter, and patience that led to our writing this book together. As I shared my story through hours of taped interviews at my office in the Black Studies Department at Portland State University, it was always with the knowledge that I was speaking to a joyously, respectfully engaged open heart and mind. I found much healing and release in telling my story. Here I must acknowledge another brilliant sisterfriend and healer, Renee Mitchell (Twysted Healing Systahs), whose invitation to participate in a day-long conference, "Redefining the Blues," provided an additional catalyst to keep going forward with this memoir and to start planning for a second one that would talk more specifically about Black women and mental health and mental illness. The journey toward healing can be difficult even for accomplished Black women in a society that does not always recognize and appreciate the full lives that we live. Overcoming the silences that doom us to spiritual and physical death is essential for recovery and survival, especially in Oregon, where a liberal and progressive white-majority culture can smother and choke off our voices.

15

    I am deeply grateful to my beloved sister Fayetta (Faye) Burch for being an anchor, a truth teller, and the first to read the manuscript that became this book. Thanks to my beloved sisterfriend Bea McMillan, who read the manuscript during our wonderful healing visit in her home in Columbus, Ohio, February 2009. Life-long sisterfriend Charlotte Rutherford provided constructive comments that helped me flesh out the story of my work around education reform in the Portland Public Schools in the 1980s. This work took me to Atlanta, Georgia, where I traveled with a dedicated and innovative educator, Joyce Harris, in order to secure the late Dr. Asa Hilliard as a consultant for the Black United Front as we developed the Portland Baseline Essays. Charlotte also prodded me to not shy away from talking about single motherhood at a time when my employment and leadership responsibilities required extensive travel. She also celebrates with me the recent success in Portland of the African American Mental Health Commission, notably the founding and opening of the Avel Gordly Center for Healing (at Oregon Health and Science University, OHSU), a clinic with a special strength in culturally specific Afrocentric services, as well as other multicultural offerings in an adult outpatient setting.

Gloria Gostnell, a dear sister and healing spirit, affirmed and confirmed that my story was worthy of being shared. She was there at the beginning of the legislative years in the early 1990s as I began to listen for my voice and discover it in the company and safety of the Black women's reading group that we formed together with Emily Bates, Beverly Johnson, Karen Powell, and Rachael Murphey. One of our first reads was bell hooks, who spoke to us about finding our voices and trusting them. Kathleen Saadat, my courageous sisterfriend-mentor-teacher-wisdom keeper, read the manuscript with deep respect and knowledge of the journey. Rupert Kinnard, whose head and heart alignment I have long admired, was a trusted male reader who loves language and music and is dearly loved by people from every walk of life. Adriene Cruz, celebrated artist, provided reminders to exercise and offered me laughter, always at the right time (and often with the right meal!). Tricia Tillman, a brilliant emerging leader, inspired me with her integrity and spirit of Harriet Tubman. My church family and faith warriors at Highland Christian Center kept me in prayer and I love and thank Rev. Dr. W. G. (Kwame) Hardy, Jr., Mother Ivy Miller, sister Gloria Franklin, sister Renee Watson Taylor, and my extended family Louise Wedge, Doris Stevenson, and Sherra Waters for their enduring love and encouragement. I acknowledge with deep gratitude my legislative aides Evelyn Crews, Sandra Herman Moose, Katy King, Sharon Hill, Yugen Rashad, Karen Powell, Denyse Peterson Wickliff, and Sean Cruz, and my dedicated legislative interns Sam Sachs and Chyerel Mayes. I hold up the names of Mrs. Pauline Bradford and Mrs. Willie Mae Hart, revered elders and mentors, and the late Honorable Judge Mercedes Deiz and Gladys McCoy. Dr. Norwood Knight-Richardson and Dr. Garfield de Bardelaben also offered support and healing advice over the years. Thanks to Kathy "Ka" Flewellen and the International Black Women's Public Policy Institute, Washington, DC.

Thanks, love, and gratitude to Senator Margaret Carter and Senator Jackie Winters—standing on the amazing shoulders of Beatrice Cannady (the first Black woman to run for elected office)—we three made history together serving in the State Senate, at the same time! Thanks to the National Organization of Black Elected Women/NOBEL Women for carrying forward the legacy and to former Rep. Jo Ann Bowman for the courage to answer the call to run to replace me in the House of Representatives.

Thanks to Dr. Harold Briggs and Dr. Joy deGruy from the African American Mental Health Commission and Portland State University School of Social Work; community builders and long-time supporters Paul and Geneva Knauls, Sam and Margaret Brooks, and Carl and Karen Talton; beloved sister warriors and mentors, Sharon Gary Smith, Iris Bell, Antoinette Edwards, and Kay Toran. To former Sen. Joan Dukes and Superintendent of Public Instruction Susan Castillo, Secretary of State Kate Brown and trusted ally former Sen. Frank Shields. To dear friends and advisers; Lolenzo Poe, James Posey and Rep. Lew Frederick; to Sen. Ted Ferrioli, Sen. Jason Atkinson, Sen. John Lim, and the late Sens. Tom Hartung and Lenn Hannon for friendship and fellowship across the aisle. And to Senate President Peter Courtney for hearing the admonishment to champion mental health reform in the state of Oregon. To all those good people from every walk of life and from all over the great State of Oregon who said an encouraging word along the way. And especially those from the old neighborhood who "lifted me as they climbed," Mrs. Willie

17

Mae Hart and Mrs. Pauline Bradford and the members of the Oregon Association of Colored Women's Clubs; and Mr. and Mrs. Maxey.

Thanks to Ed Washington, former Metro Councillor, and Jim Hill, former State Treasurer, both for sound political advice; with deep appreciation to Roy Jay and Baruti Artharee for friendship, encouragement, and always having my back; and to the beloved late Gladys McCoy, former Multnomah County Chair, and the late Bill McCoy, former State Senator, for encouragement, insight, wisdom, and blazing the trail.

I am thankful to my colleagues in the Black Studies Department at Portland State University, who provided me with so much encouragement over the last two years: Dr. E. Kofi Agorsah, Dr. Darrell Millner, Turiya Autry, Clare Washington, Dr. Pedro Ferbel-Azcarate, Walidah Imarisha, Dr. Ethan Johnson, Dr. Joseph Smith-Buani, Dr. Dalton Miller-Jones, Angela Canton, and my remarkable teaching assistant and legislative intern Meggin Clay. Many thanks and honor to The Skanner News Group and the *Portland Observer* newspaper for remarkable coverage of legislative activities over many years that has informed, educated, and enlightened Oregonians to the concerns of African American Oregonians. I am deeply grateful to all the members of the Black United Front and the leadership of the late Rev. John Jackson, Ronnie Herndon, and Richard Brown. I also pay tribute to the Urban League of Portland and to the American Friends Service Committee and the American Leadership Forum. I am a product of all of these great organizations. They provided me with the best community-based teachings on how to become an effective organizer and how to be a servant leader, unapologetically in service to all people, especially Black people.

A.L.G.
Portland, Oregon
August 2010

CHAPTER ONE

Before We Become Dust

Growing up, finding my own voice was tied up with denying my voice or having it forcefully rejected and in all of that the memory of my father is very strong. To this day—and I am today a very experienced public speaker—preparation to speak takes a great deal of energy. A lot of the energy is dedicated to overcoming fear and the pain of injury previously inflicted on me for speaking up. Over the years, I have developed some sure ways to find my voice, catch my breath, and start to speak. Sometimes I think prayerfully of the names of my mother, Beatrice Bernice Gordly, and of my grandmothers, Alberta Louise Randolph and Lessie Gordly. Sometimes I say their names to myself, sometimes I speak them aloud. I say the names with thanks and gratitude to God. Saying their names always centers me. Sometimes I even start my remarks by dedicating my words to honor their memory. I also use word-for-word prepared texts for my speeches, not just notes or outlines. I have to write down every word to get through my fear.

Just recently at an Urban League dinner in town, Dr. Julianne Malveaux, the brilliant economist, gave a wonderful speech—without notes! I've loved listening to her for many years. I admire how she uses language, her comfort in her own skin, her way of storytelling, and her use of humor. As I acknowledge and affirm who she is, a little piece of *me* still feels "not good enough." A tape recording in my head about being "not good enough" was violently enforced in my life over a period of many years. My story involves a struggle to quiet that tape and find my own voice in the world. Though we are both accomplished Black women and share certain perspectives and experiences, my voice is different from Dr. Malveaux's. We have different, unique stories and selves, formed in different, unique circumstances. My circumstances took shape in Portland, Oregon, where I was born on February 13, 1947.

Many, many times during my childhood my mom, my sister Faye, and I would be at home glued to the television set watching something related to the Civil Rights Movement. In fact, any time a Black person was on television at all my mom would be on the phone calling someone to tune in and watch—or someone would be calling her—which speaks volumes about Black invisibility in the early 1960s. The Rev. Dr. Martin Luther King, Jr., visited Vancouver Avenue Baptist Church in November 1961. My grandmother's copy of his book about the Montgomery Bus Boycott, *Stride Toward Freedom*, was signed in that church when he came to visit. I have this volume in my personal collection, a treasured memento of those historic years of hope and struggle.

A march held in Portland on September 22, 1963, brought the Civil Rights Movement even more directly home to me in Oregon. A wonderful high school teacher, Mr. Amasa Gilman, encouraged me and my friends to participate in this march, intended to protest the murder of the four little girls in church in Birmingham, Alabama. On that Sunday, we marched from Vancouver Avenue Baptist Church on the east side into downtown Portland and we massed in front of the federal courthouse. I have a strong memory of being present with my girlfriends Irma and Lela, my buddies. We were sisterfriends and traveled everywhere together. Many participants in the march spoke about their pain over the killings. It was painful for me to dwell on this outrage but it was also a relief. That march was a defining moment because it exposed me to people who spoke out in support of something of great importance—civil rights—and against something horrible—the murder of innocent children. Looking back, the event allowed me to link the issue of African American civil rights explicitly to horrendous violence against black girls. Something about that moment in time remains heavy for me to this day. Yet that march told me that I could have a voice, too, even as a young person.

The march evokes important memories of the power of words in my life. Words carry so much feeling, history, and meaning. Words carry the power to inspire; they can also inflict great pain. I always attend carefully to language because I want my words to mean what

I say. I'm keenly aware that words are not just sent, they are also received, yet the speaker can only control the first part, the sending. In my life, all too often the right word from me did not bring the desired response. I remember an assignment in high school—it may have been a crossword puzzle—requiring us to identify names of famous people. One name was that of the well-known film director Elia Kazan. I knew the name because I was a reader and the name was just there for me. When I spoke out the answer in class, the teacher looked at me and asked: "How do you know that?" I felt like I had been struck because his words meant: "You are not supposed to know that." Many years later a white female colleague in the legislature would say to me with surprise, after hearing me speak: "You sound smart!" A boundary between knowledge and speech had been transgressed and this teacher reprimanded me for assuming the power to cross it.

At school, knowing the right word and speaking it often elicited racist hostility. At home, I faced another set of challenges related to speaking up. Talking back, especially to my father, was strictly forbidden. My dad let my sister and me know that we were not to question him or ask "Why?" about anything. When he spoke, that was The Law. A defining moment of enforcing this Law took place in the kitchen, when I was a teenager. My mom was fixing dinner and she and my dad were talking. I was sitting in a chair; somehow I was part of the conversation and asked the question "Why?" The next thing I knew I was picking myself up from the floor. My father had struck me across the face so hard that I literally saw stars. That punishment was for asking the question "Why?"

It is a gift to look back and unpack everything in between then and now and reflect aloud. How many of us get to do that before we become dust?

REFERENCES

Burrell, Raymond, III. *A History of Vancouver Avenue Baptist Church*. Portland, 2009.

"Live as One or Perish As Fools, Warning Given by Dr. King Here," *Oregon Journal*, 9 November 1961.

"Portlanders Join Rights March," *The Oregonian*, 23 September 1963.

CHAPTER TWO

Our Day Will Come

Throughout my school years, the association between speech and power—and punishment—was strong. I was a reader at home and I can remember being called on to stand in front of the class to read in grade school. Sometimes, a teacher would select a member of the class to take a ruler and hit the hands of other students for punishment. At least once, I was selected for that role. I distinctly recall the feeling of power it gave me and that I recoiled from that feeling.

Other measurements and punishments were meted out during my grade school years. I remember being self-conscious about my short hair; my sister's hair was longer. I remember being teased at school for having short hair. A beauty standard, or being considered "cute," was tied to whether the girl's hair was straight or kinky, short or long. I knew I was not in the category of "cute" and in grade school I started to think of myself as unattractive. But I found safety in books and reading and in disappearing that way. I felt acceptance with my close girlfriends like Anna Cruz and Beverly Griffin from the neighborhood. And I knew my mother thought that my sister and I were very special. I knew it from the way she talked with us and the way in which she shared her affection and hugs. She loved to dress me and my sister up in little dresses and she always had a camera and took our pictures. But that affirmation all but disappeared once I went outside our door. In fact, there was a little girl across the street who was bigger than me, Jeanette, who beat me up regularly on the way to school. Perhaps had my older brother Tyrone been around, I might have had protection, but he left home to join the Air Force just before I ended elementary school, when he was seventeen.

My sister and I attended Girls Polytechnic High School, which no longer exists. My mother was insistent that we both attend Girls Poly even though Jefferson High School was the neighborhood school, within just a few blocks' walking distance from our home. She wanted us to get a good education. There was a rigorous admission process and grade point average requirement at Girls Poly. The school was divided into a college track and a vocational track. My mom wanted us to have access to the college track. I don't think it was ever spoken but I believe she also wanted to keep us away from boys. She was focused on getting her daughters a good education even if it took us out of the neighborhood, so we applied and were accepted. A few other girls in our neighborhood also went to Girls Poly, like Anna Cruz and Charlotte Rivers, and we had a ritual of getting together and walking to school in the mornings. We walked all the way from our home on North Williams Avenue to N.E. 24th and Everett Street. There was fun and adventure in our walks, and time for talking and socializing.

The student body at Girls Poly was around five hundred total; my graduating class of 1965 numbered fewer than one hundred. My neighborhood classmates and I talked regularly about our feeling of alienation, and the sense that we were in a hostile environment at school. I wanted to take the "Business Machines" course—which at the time meant typing, primarily—and the teacher of that course let me know that it was a waste of time since there wouldn't be any job opportunities for the colored girls with those skills after graduation. My mother advocated for me to be able to take that course. When I started at Girls Poly I wanted to be a nurse. The nursing school I had my eye on was at Emanuel Hospital and they did not allow Black students until the 1970s. So Business Machines was already my second choice in a school environment that pushed Jim Crow on Black students in our training and employment. My guidance counselor also insisted that Business Machines was a waste of my time and pushed me towards Commercial Foods. That track included courses in cooking and job placement in that field. With my mom's support I avoided Commercial Foods and was able to enroll in Business Machines.

Jim Crow at school made Girls Poly a painful journey. Black girls' voices were actively silenced. Mrs. Martin, the vice principal, told my friends and me in the hallway that we were too loud and that we should be quiet. She also was the one who banned Black music from the school talent show. Years later, while I was running for office, Mrs. Martin was one of the leaders of a women's organization that had a role in endorsing candidates. As I sat in the endorsement meeting, it dawned on me who she was, and anger and shame came up in my body. In that meeting, I contemplated reminding her of who I was and, more importantly, of who she was: part of the problem of racism in the public schools. I did not do so in the moment but afterwards I did share with my sister my strong reaction to seeing her. There are still folks around in Portland in roles of influence who are part of the historic white supremacist barriers enforced against African Americans. Enforcing those barriers in public school deeply harms tender and impressionable young minds.

What made school tolerable was my connection to a family of girls from the neighborhood. We all hung together and took care of each other and encouraged one another. Yet Girls Poly remained alien, unwelcoming territory. When John F. Kennedy was murdered I was in drama class. Someone came in to tell our teacher the news. I remember the shock and tears; we all cried. Yet a white girl in the class sniped out loud that "a nigger did it." Anna Cruz—one of the girls from our neighborhood group—jumped up and grabbed that girl and they started fighting. Then we were put in kind of a lock-down situation in the basement. I remember being held there as if in jail. The words "a nigger did it" just went to my heart. It was just such a horrible, horrible thought. I also remember a lot of time spent in front of the television set at home during that time. I remember my mother watching and paying very close attention to everything that was going on and so my sister and I did, too. It was a very emotional time with lots of tears. My school memory of Kennedy's assassination remains very painful.

On a brighter note, I remember enjoying the Business Machines class. The enjoyment was in knowing that I could perform well. I remember the satisfaction. Later I got a job working with Pacific Northwest Bell, the old phone company, working with computers. I went back to the Business Machines teacher, Mrs. Waller, and I let her know that contrary to the messages given to me at Girls Poly I had a found an excellent job at the phone company. I got satisfaction out of going back to share that with her and setting the record straight.

I don't really know my mom's personal story about her education. I do remember that when I got a typewriter she was very interested! I used to practice typing at home and it was a big deal. Mom wanted to type and I encouraged her. My memory of seeing my mom at the typewriter is my first vision of her doing something connected to furthering her own education. It was summertime and we picked beans and berries; that work brought in money to purchase the typewriter. It was a Royal, in a brown case.

A positive high school teacher who stands out in memory is Mrs. Matthews, an English teacher. She encouraged us to "read everything!" That message fit me perfectly. I was a reader—like my mother. She kept stacks of magazines like *Readers Digest* and *Ebony* and newspapers on the living room table. I was the kid at home who wanted to sit at the dining table with something to read, even if it was just the cereal box at breakfast. I remember being told that I could read after mealtime in a very loving way, in a way that acknowledged that I loved to read. I have a warm memory of Mrs. Matthews. I ran into her many, many years later at Lloyd Center Mall. She was a bit hunched over with age but she was still Mrs. Matthews and I felt warmth and affirmation in my memory of her younger self.

School memories are connected to words and my love of words. I loved hearing words spoken by others and studying how other people used language. I remember preparing feverishly for a major spelling test and I got all the words right, except for one. The word I missed was "zeros." To this day I can't spell "zeros"! I was disappointed that I didn't get them all correct but still satisfied that only one of them got away—and a "zero," at that. I just had a thing about words. Art class provided unexpected pleasure, as it was shielded a bit from the pressure of getting skills for future employment and the shadow of Jim Crow. I loved to sit down and work with the paint and paintbrushes or mold clay. I recall modeling a clay Adam and Eve in the Garden of Eden with a serpent between them and painting a picture of slaves picking cotton. I have a fond memory of getting in touch with that creative side of myself in high school. Looking back, I think my choice of subjects in art reflected a need to fill a void at school, especially a need to fill in the history of slavery that was missing in my studies.

Another space for making choices about learning involved the library. My mom, sister, and I each had library cards. We checked out books regularly. Grandmother Randolph, my mother's mother, also had lots of books. My uncles Lawrence and Clarence had a collection of little pocketbooks on different subjects, and whenever my sister and I stayed at my grandmother's home, we loved to get into that collection of books. There were also comic books and we read everything from Little LuLu, to Nancy, to Superman. My grandmother also subscribed to *Ebony, Jet, The Crisis*, and *Sepia Magazine* (published in Texas). I still have her magazines from the forties and fifties and her copy of *Up From Slavery* by Booker T. Washington. Grandmother Randolph's dining room table was full of her reading. Books, magazines, mail, church bulletins: everything had its place. My mother had a similar table piled with reading material in our home when I was growing up and now I have that same table. And so does my sister!

It wasn't until I attended Portland State University and took classes in the Black Studies Department that I was exposed to the great works of African American literature. I remember getting very angry when I discovered this body of writing that I previously didn't know existed. There had clearly been a huge omission in my public school education. Nonetheless, I knew about Black heroes like Washington, Phillis Wheatley, and Harriet Tubman. My grandmother had a prominent role in naming her local women's club for Tubman and she passed that powerful knowledge along to me.

My first favorite book was *Gone with the Wind*. I had my own hardback edition. I was taken with all the characters—and with the fact that it was a big thick book. I liked the big ones that took time to get through! Big books gave me personal space and private time with language. That book was like a treasure. I even took pleasure in turning the pages. Later, seeing the movie, hearing the words aloud, and seeing the story come alive was a powerful experience. Looking back I think that book was a way into Southern speech ways and the history of slavery for me, elements of culture and the past that I only had partial access to from my family and not at all from public school. As late as 2005, a young teen-aged girl spoke up at a community meeting in Portland about still not knowing "our history," with its roots in slavery and Africa; I wrote about this devastating omission in *The New York Times* to underscore the urgency of culturally competent, non-racist education for all our children, in every community.

My mother was a letter writer and a card sender. I distinctly remember receiving the first letter she ever wrote to me when I

27

Seated, from left to right, Lessie Gordly, Alberta Louise Randolph, and Evelyn Dowell. Standing, James Dowell (Alberta's son). Portland, Oregon, c. 1958

went to Africa for the first time during college. She had beautiful handwriting. Mom loved sending Christmas cards and she kept a list of all the cards she received each year. There was an annual ritual of mom sending her cards out. She was the one who remembered birthdays and anniversaries. I wish I could say I carried that practice forward! Mom kept a stack of cards as they arrived at holiday time. My sister and I loved putting them up on the entryway door as decoration. As we ran out of space in the living room we'd move on to the door in the kitchen ... and then on to the archway between the living room and dining room. I remember marveling at the number of friends my parents had from other places in the United States far beyond Portland. I can still see my mother sitting at the dining room table with the box of cards and the list and her little book of addresses and phone numbers, just going through them one by one. Like *Gone with the Wind*, the holiday cards pointed to a world of feeling and history far beyond my small child's world of Portland, Oregon.

Our little girls' world was constrained yet social, along certain lines. When I was around ten years old, I got to invite all my little girlfriends to a birthday party at the house. It was a big deal. It was a big deal for my mother, who always delighted in doing things with and for "her girls." She received great enjoyment in the planning of activities and in watching us enjoy ourselves. When we were in high school, we did not go to a lot of parties. One party does stand out: that of my friend Irma Brown's. Somehow Irma got to have this party and we got to go, most likely because Irma's folks were church-going people. It was a special occasion. I remember the food and all of us dancing in her living room to "It's Your Thing" by the Isley Brothers. Like my mother and father, I loved to dance.

Irma Brown, Lela Triplet, and I had a singing group. We had one and only one performance: at the mothers' and daughters' tea at Girls Poly. The song that we chose was "Our Day Will Come," a number one hit in 1963 by Ruby and the Romantics. We practiced, and practiced, and practiced—in stairwells at school and away from school, too. Somehow I wound up being the lead singer. Irma was a wonderful seamstress and made all our matching dresses. They were shiny blue brocade and we wore heels. We had special hair-dos and we were very "The Supremes" in our fashion style. We sang at the tea in front of the whole school with our mothers present. For years I carried forward the warm memory of our mothers' pride in us on that occasion. When I ran into Lela's mom decades later, she still called up her vivid memory of the three of us singing "Our Day Will Come." That song is about romantic love but the words allowed us to express hope and yearning that resonated far beyond romance. Like reading words in important books, singing the words of popular songs by Black artists together with my girlfriends for our loving and appreciative mothers nourished my belief in the power of language.

REFERENCES
Washington, Booker T. *Up From Slavery: An Autobiography.* New York: Doubleday, Page, 1901.
Mitchell, Margaret. *Gone With the Wind.* New York: The Macmillan Company, 1936.
Gordly, Avel. "Oregon Cultural Competency: We Need to Know Our History." http://www.nytimes.com/ref/college/coll-opinions-gordly.html (2005).

CHAPTER THREE

"It is Better to Be Loved than Feared"
—African Proverb

I attended high school with my sister for two years. Like most sisters close in age we fought about things that, looking back, were so silly—mostly about clothes. We shared a room and a closet. Aside from this normal squabbling we took care of each other because of my dad. We were usually punished at the same time by my father. His way of disciplining us was to beat us. These were beatings, not spankings. We had to go outside and pick a branch from the snowball tree (mom's favorite) ourselves, bring it inside, and then receive our punishment. Sometimes he would use a cord or his belt. Today they would call his treatment of us child abuse and he'd be behind bars or we'd be in foster care. These very, very severe punishments made us fear him. I also remember being a protector of my sister. I have a memory of standing between him and her and letting him know that he'd better not hit her. I have memories of our little quiet sisterly conversations in the bedroom we shared. My sister remembers running away to Grandma Randolph's house to avoid being beaten. I ran away but only to the backyard. I still dream about the closet in our room where I also hid. When I ran from my father, I did not get as far away as my sister.

We lived with a lot of fear of my father; fear of the beatings and also fear of his voice. My father judged our behavior in terms of obedience around the house and school grades. He made it clear that we could not bring Cs home. Occasionally we'd go on family outings, like to Multnomah Falls in the Columbia River Gorge. He liked to do things like that. But fear of my father created a barrier for me to get to know him as well as for him to get to know me. My sister would say the same thing. When my father was gone on a railroad run my mother corrected us with words; only occasionally did she say, "Get the switch" for physical punishment. Generally things around the house waited until my dad returned from his railroad run. Then there would be a reciting of the wrongs of the two girls and discipline followed.

My brother left home because he and my father did not get along. Their relationship was emotionally and physically violent. My brother left at the earliest age possible to join the Air Force, with an uncle, Lawrence. He escaped! My parents did not know of his plans. He was just gone one day. For the longest time, my sister and I felt that we had done something to drive my brother away from home. It was years later that we learned that it was conflict between him and Dad that created the rift. I never knew of or witnessed the details of Tyrone's conflicts with my father. In terms of its violence, my guess is that my father was doing what was done to him. Dad also enforced The Law: "don't speak unless you are spoken to" and "don't talk back." So if my brother was doing either of those things, and I'm sure he was, that would have resulted in tussles.

My own memories of Tyrone are not especially rosy. He was nine years older than me and sometimes he was left in charge of his sisters. One time, Tyrone and his friend Linell decided they were going to torture me. They poured a glass of vinegar and made some buttered toast and forced me to drink the vinegar and eat the

31

My father Fay Lee Gordly and my brother Tyrone Lee Gordly

Faye and me at the N. Williams Avenue house, c. 1957.

buttered toast. Still, I used to like to hang out with him. He had toys I liked, like an erector set, and he had a bike. Sometimes he had to take me with him. Once I got my foot stuck in the back spokes of the bike while riding with him. I mainly remember being in the way of my brother's fun with the fellas.

Tyrone's empty room was a reminder that he was gone. It was like a hole in our home and in our family. The room also had a doorway entrance to what we called the play porch or the sunroom. The sunroom had dual access through a door in Tyrone's room and another one in my sister's and my room. After time his room became kind of a catchall; my mother would store things in there. But in our younger years, we almost didn't want to open that door because it was the reminder that someone was missing.

During his time away, Tyrone kept contact with my mother, though I'm not sure how regularly. He may have phoned. I know that his departure created a period of depression and grief for my mother. For years, Tyrone's leaving was the backdrop of everything for her. In the early 1970s, when I was a student at Portland State and he had been gone for thirteen years, I appointed myself family emissary and decided that I was going to track my brother down. We knew he was in New York City and that, after leaving the Air Force, he had lived with another uncle, James, who helped him land work with the post office. I made this trip with the intent of having him come back and visit. Tyrone was living in Hempstead, New York; Uncle James was in Queens. We had a very special reunion together in New York and then, not long afterwards, my brother came home to Portland.

Tyrone's return was a huge, huge time of joy for my mother. My mother came to life. She was always gracious and smiling but with her son home she just lit up. She beamed. From that point forward, he came home just about every year. The contact between us became regular and that was a very good thing. When Tyrone returned after his long absence, he and my dad kind of walked around each other as if on eggshells. But over time, they found their peace. My brother eventually convinced my dad to travel with him back to New York to visit with some of the family and to see the big city through his eyes. That was huge! The family story is that my dad wanted to take seven hats on this trip—one for every day of the week! There was no talking him out of the hats. Later we buried him with a favorite hat and the Union Pacific's Golden Spike plaque that he received upon retirement from the railroad.

I'm dimly aware that, during my teen years, my mom would retreat to her bedroom with the door closed. This memory has left me to wonder: was she depressed? If so, my brother's absence I believe was a likely catalyst. There were times when she just disappeared. I never had a sense that my mom was losing patience with me or my sister or that we were in her way. Today I can acknowledge that she was complicit in my father's brutal behavior toward us. Sometimes when the beatings were so bad I may have felt disappointment or anger that she didn't step in or stop it or speak up for us. I remember welts and bruising on my body. I remember a lot of tears, a lot of crying. My sister and I would be in our bedroom just sobbing and sobbing and sobbing.

Another stand-out memory connected to our bedroom is of the night our house caught on fire. Our house had a coal-burning furnace. My sister and I were responsible for throwing coal in the basement from an opening in the back of the house. Cinders from the coal may have caught the roof shingles on fire. The part of the house that burned most was around our bedroom. I don't remember who came up to get us up out of bed but the person told us that we had to get out of the house. I remember standing out on the sidewalk, looking up at our house in flames. My sister and I couldn't use our room for quite a while after that, while the damage was being repaired.

There was a period of time when my father drank. The sequence is unclear in my memory but my sense is that some of the beatings we kids endured happened when he had been drinking, though not all of them. I have no memory that my mother was ever threatened or beaten by my father. Quite the contrary. I observed them to be playful with one another. A lot of their play took place around food. My father loved to cook and he and mom would sometimes be in the kitchen together cooking up a pot of chili. Dad loved enchiladas, too, and Tex-Mex cooking, from his Texas roots, no doubt. If he went fishing he'd bring home a mess of fish and my mom would clean them and cook them. My parents also entertained a lot in our home and went to the homes of their friends. They had a real social life and

my memory is that they had a lot of good times with one another. My father was a talker and teller of tall tales. Given his regular absence from home, he may have had a fling or two outside of marriage. Overall, however, my parents' way of interacting was playful.

Two pictures of my mother and father

 convey something to me about their marriage. One picture, taken in the 1940s, is of my mom and dad in their youth and the other is at their last wedding anniversary together, their forty-fourth. The joy on their faces is the same in both pictures. Viewing these pictures again recently I realized that the image of my parents' smiling faces is the picture I saw all my life, and it shapes my sense of their union. My mom and dad liked to dance around the house together. I have vivid memories of their dancing; sometimes my sister and I danced with them. Dad would have his favorite records on—he brought back a lot of the "sounds" or music from his runs to Chicago and Kansas City—and we'd all be dancing in the living room, doing our thing. I have similarly light-hearted memories of my parents' entertaining their friends in our home.

My parents lived together for over forty years and it required a great deal of patience on my mother's part. My sense of her patience derives from memories of her way of getting my father to think twice about something. Many times I heard my mother say "Now Fay …" or simply "Oh, be quiet," always said with love. It was her way of grounding him. I never heard my mother express anger at my father; annoyance but not anger. She had an abundance of patience; I don't know that it was masking other feelings. I think they found a way to be with one another. I'm also sure my father heard it plenty from folks in the community—including his mother-in-law—that he was really lucky to have my mother for a wife. And he *was* very lucky. I was also aware of admonishments from my maternal grandmother to the effect that she had raised an eyebrow concerning his suitability as a husband for her daughter. I'm sure my dad heard that my mom was too good for him because I certainly heard it. I'm not quite sure what "too good" meant but my dad was known to be a rascal.

Mom was smart and beautiful. Part of my mother's attraction to my father was that he was a great dancer; she enjoyed dancing. And they continued to dance throughout their marriage—all those trips around the living room! They obviously enjoyed each other's company.

My parents married in 1939; my brother Tyrone was born that same year. My father's mother, Lessie Gordly, worked as a domestic in Portland and then she worked in the shipyards during the war. Prior to coming here, the Gordlys lived on a farm in Texas. As far as I know, my father's dad worked that farm; family members also picked cotton for seasonal wages. My mother's mother also did domestic work. She married three times, first to a man named Dowell, then Coleman, and lastly to Gillespie Randolph, who worked on the railroad. It's possible that there was an earlier marriage before Dowell that I have not heard about. Given my own marital history, I often believe I'm trying to keep up with my Grandmother Randolph!

People called Gillespie Randolph "Ran" for short. I knew him growing up. I have a strong memory of him watching TV as an elderly man, especially the Lawrence Welk show, of which he was a great fan. Since he carried the name of the famous trumpet player Dizzy Gillespie, I always wondered at his admiration for Welk. I spent enough time in my grandparents' home to have a very clear memory of Ran and Lawrence Welk, as I do of my grandmother's love of reading and the many books she kept around. When we visited Grandma Randolph, her husband had his room, the living room, with the television on and she made sure we girls always had the opportunity to read in another part of the house. She always spoke to us about some new idea or event that she herself had read about.

I have no memory of Grandmother Lessie's husband. My dad talked a little about their life in Texas, especially about Lessie's mother, who had light skin. It was understood that she was related to people from England, and once she had a relative come visit the house who was white. This person's appearance at the house caused a sensation; they were just stunned that this person was all white.

Fragments of the story as I remember it include people running around the house in a strong reaction to this person's presence. Given the harshness of the color line in those days, the family was understandably agitated. If the wrong people saw this transgression of Jim Crow, it could endanger their lives. I don't think my father's father ever made a trip to Portland.

My sense of my parents' courtship is tied to the growth of the African American community in Portland during the World War II era, when thousands migrated to work in the shipyards. There were lots of clubs and places where young Black people got together, especially in the area around Williams Avenue, Russell Street, and Broadway, and some parts of Vancouver Avenue, too. Social outlets and activities included live shows by the great big-band musicians of the time, many of whom passed through Portland on their way to Seattle or California. Folks of my mom and dad's age were caught up in jazz and the blues; they were out there enjoying it all; my dad was twenty-five when World War II broke out, my mother twenty-one. I do not have a clear story about my parents' courtship but I do have vivid memories of their membership in a core group of married couples, almost a club of its own. The husbands all worked on the railroad with my dad; the wives maybe worked part time and maintained the home front, raising the kids. They attended church together and socialized together in the setting of Portland's night life and music scene as well as in each others' homes. These were life-long friendships. Their lives were also very much about the music.

My father finished high school; my mom did not. He attended Phillis Wheatley High School in Texas and played football. He was very proud of some of the folks who graduated from that school who had gone on to do great and good things, especially one man from New York, a politician, Percy Sutton, whose name he brought up regularly at home. Although it is clear to me that Grandma Randolph regarded my dad as a rascal, he nonetheless stayed with his family, took care of his family, and performed all the requirements of manhood at that time. My dad was someone who worked hard but was street wise, someone who would do whatever was necessary to make sure that his family was taken care of.

My mom and dad loved each other. In their own way they found a way to forgive one another when they needed to do that. Somehow they found their way to a lot of laughter and their own way of truth telling. They stayed together. I only remember one time, when I was little, that my dad threatened to leave the house. It happened in the living room. I remember me saying something like "Oh, please don't leave!" and feeling like I had to do something so that we all stayed together. Whatever that was, we got over it, because my dad never left.

Our home was at 4511 North Williams Avenue. (My sister, brother, and I still own this home and make it available as a rental.) We were a working-class family in a working-class neighborhood. Growing up I was aware of times of real financial struggle in the household, like not having enough money to pay the mortgage. In my child's mind I'd think: "What can I do to help?" But we always had enough food. I seem to recall struggles around clothing. There was a neighbor, Mrs. Slaughter, who gave my mom some shoes for my sister and me one year. I remember her as someone who looked out after my sister and me and also the other kids growing up on the block. My mom did part-time work from time to time. My dad was not happy about her working outside of the home. She clerked in Neighborhood Bill's grocery store. An African American man, Mr. Bill Benton, owned the store and hired people from the neighborhood. At one point she worked in a drugstore; and she also worked in a club called the "Dude Ranch." Local musicians and even famous traveling musicians of the time would stop through. I remember pictures of Mom dressed in her work uniform—a cowgirl getup with boots!

My mother's beauty was a subject of constant discussion. She was a great beauty from the Lena Horne school, that is, light-skinned and long-haired. Upon meeting her, everyone would comment on what a beautiful, graceful person she was. And it went beyond just the physical beauty; they meant her spirit, the person that she was. My dad's male friends teased him regularly, saying that he'd really done well—maybe too well—in marrying her. Dad and Mom used to have card parties at our house. My dad and his cronies would be at the table; there would be big pots of food—always chili—and cards and gambling. My sister and I would find our way to the top of the stairs—sometimes creeping as far down as we could get in order to see and hear—until we got caught and were chased back upstairs. The next day we would look under the dining-room table for loose change and go to the kitchen for left-over goodies from the night before. Sometimes we overheard remarks about our parents' relationship.

Some of the commentary we overheard concerned social class and skin color. As I've noted my mom was light-skinned and considered a very beautiful woman. I remember lots of comments about how fortunate my dad was to be married to her, like she was a prize he had won and should cherish. In my girlhood years, tensions around my own physical appearance and around my father's stern ways with us children made it painful for me to hear that I resembled him. I would hear from family that I looked like my father and that my sister looked like my mother.

Because my dad's work on the railroad took him out of the house for two or three days at a time my mother was our day-to-day protector. My memory is that when something happened to us at school that went against how she felt we should be treated, she would show up. But when my father came home off the road, there was a significant shift and a rise in tension in the house. My mom and we daughters had our rituals that did not include him, whether we were popping beans together, watching the pot, picking blackberries for blackberry cobbler, or baking gingerbread—that I can still smell to this day. When Dad came home, I felt he interrupted our rituals. He had his ways and concerns about our performance. "How ya doing in school?" he'd ask. We could not get Cs. He was attentive to how we were behaving in the community and to whether or not we were embarrassing the family. We could not attend parties like most of our friends did and my sister and I were restricted in our movements outside the house.

Not only was there an emotional split in our home life between Dad being home and not, but as my sister and I grew, Faye's connection to our mom became distinct from mine. She was the extrovert; I was the introvert, and perceived as less social. I'd say the two of them were closer. They had more in common and always seemed to me to be sharing something I did not have access to. For example, my sister and mother became shopping buddies; I did not like to go shopping. They developed rituals of womanhood that I did not share. This situation left me feeling more vulnerable to my dad.

Dad's mother, Lessie Gordly, was also our protector. She was aware of my sister's and my fear of our father. We told on my dad to her. Words passed between my grandmother and my father about his behavior toward us. Whenever my sister and I were in her presence, we always felt safe.

I have a sense that something went on between my father's dad and his sons. When my dad's brother Eddie came to Portland, he got into a lot of trouble in the community. My sister and I came across a letter from the Improved and Benevolent Protective Order of Elks of the World dated in the late 1930s to Lessie asking her to keep him away from the lodge. He had been causing a scene and had brought a knife into the building. My dad also had his rough side. We knew he had a gun. We also heard murmurs in the community about him being streetwise. In addition, Dad was an auxiliary policeman with the Portland Police Bureau, part of a "crew of black men" hired to police certain events.

Grandma Lessie's home on North Ivy Street (and later, North Rodney Street) was our second home. We ate there regularly. She would also bring home her "famous" shopping bag of goodies for us girls, some of which came from the houses of the wealthy white people she worked for in the West Hills and Laurelhurst. She was quite a cook. She had desserts covered: jello molds, cakes, pies. She was also very careful in her dress and appearance, for church or any other occasion. When I see Grandma Lessie in a photograph, I know I look like her. I prefer to see my resemblance to my beloved grandmother than to see what I'm usually told: that I look like my father. Then again, my father looks like Grandma Lessie, so what am I going to say!

I have blocked out a great deal of childhood memories. My sister can remember details of events right down to what people were wearing. I was present but I just don't have the memory. I was in my own head. We were under the same roof at the same time but I blocked out so much. I vividly remember my grandmother Lessie's death, however. I was twelve or thirteen. It was a huge, huge loss. Something was gone that I never gave voice to. We would call it abandonment now. The year was 1959. She had a stroke and was hospitalized. I did not see her in the hospital. My father took her to Texas for burial. I don't remember attending a funeral. It was a time of sorrow for us all. Her passing was very hard on my father. They were close; he called her "mama." For me, it was like a disappearance. One day she was there and then she was gone.

A few years ago, I went to San Antonio for a conference. It was the National Conference of State Legislators and I spent some time in a library archives trying to find my grandmother's burial site. I did not find it but I did find her birth record and my dad's father's birth record and some other information. Someday I hope to locate her gravesite. My sister and I came upon some family materials recently, including letters from a woman friend of Lessie's offering guidance about her love life (which surprised us!) and other letters from relatives. There is a hint in some of these letters that we may have had a family member who spent time in an asylum; I remain very interested to know about any history of mental illness in the family and it yet may be possible to track it down through letters.

My father's way of being present with his daughters was stern but when I think about the tone of our family life, my mind is drawn to the influence of my grandmothers and my mother collectively. Everything they poured into both my sister and me shaped my life choices in every respect, about friendship, men, and community roles. I was and remain greatly influenced by the women in the family.

Church was definitely a training ground for me, although we did not realize it at the time. We were all given roles as young people. The pastor's wife, Mrs. Lee, used to come and pick my sister and me up and take us to church when Mom was doing something else. My grandmothers and Mrs. Lee had a strong bond around children. Today I understand what they and other women of that generation poured into me. They were my role models. I didn't sing in the choir but I was in the little church clubs and young peoples' organizations. One time I was selected to speak and introduce some kind of children's program. Mrs. Evelyn Harris was in charge and she was very intentionally grooming us young ladies; she believed in us and let us know how much she believed in us. In my presentation I was supposed to say her name but I turned it around and said "Harris Evelyn." My main memory from that day is having made a mistake publicly. I felt like I placed a blemish on the whole program; somehow I had that burden on my shoulders. To this day, I am conscious of how I wanted to disappear and run out of there that Sunday long ago.

My mother's family was very church oriented and active in the women's clubs of the time. Grandma Randolph was one of the founders of the Oregon Association of Colored Women's Clubs and one of the founders of Portland's Harriet Tubman Club. My mother and her two sisters, Birdie Mae and Esther, were all beautiful young girls, just to-die-for beauties. They were well thought of and came from a hard-working family. Birdie Mae and Esther died at a young age, before they reached thirty-five, one, I believe, of pneumonia.

The only image I have of my mother's father is from a picture I had in my family collection of a guy in a sharp suit carrying a gun. I had this picture when my first cousin Mel Bailey came to Portland a few years ago, seeking information about his father, who he learned was one of the Duke brothers, a family of community builders. Mel was the son of my mother's sister Esther and had been given away as a baby. I also had a picture of his mother in my collection. Turns out my mother's father's name was Melvin and cousin Mel is named after this man in the sharp suit with the gun. I don't have a sense of Grandfather Melvin other than he was somebody that you did not mess with.

Grandma Lessie, Dad's mom, truly loved my mom and really looked after her. She also took my sister and me under her wing. When she was aware that we were hurting in some way, she tried to smooth things over with my dad. She also advocated for us, reminding him to do things like take us girls to the dentist. He never did. Sadly, I have a whole world of terrible stories around seeing the dentist as an adult, compounded by this early neglect of my teeth. One time, a white male dentist said hurtful racist things to me while I was sitting in the chair and unable to move. I was frozen to the spot and literally had no voice. It was a traumatizing experience and affected me for a long, long, long time. For years I avoided dental treatment because of this experience and my dental health has suffered from further neglect. That memory sits next to another in my mind, from my teenage years. I was eighteen or nineteen and went to a clinic in the neighborhood. A white male doctor suggested that I—and all black women—should have their tubes tied and should not be having babies. Both of these experiences in memory conjure up shame and the perennially unanswered question: Why is such animus and venom being directed at me? For too long, I thought their racism had to do with something about me. I did not talk to anybody else about these experiences at the time. Nor did I have the tools to figure it all out for many years.

When my mom passed away, Dad was lost, literally lost. He was depressed for a time. He developed a mantra or lament that he said over and over again for over twenty years after she passed: "Why did God take her? Why not me? Why did he take the good one?" He'd go on about how she was too good for him and that my sister and I should not think that he really did anything to raise us because she did it all. He let us know in his own way that he really loved this woman. He never married again. He had a girlfriend here or there (as much as my sister would allow!). My strongest memories of growing

43

up in our family are of my mother's patience and of my sister and I "waiting for the other shoe to drop." We were just kind of skating along.

Nonetheless, my mom doted on her girls. My mom affirmed my reading; she knew I loved to read. She also bought me a couple of diaries over the years because she remembered that I liked to keep a diary. I had a sewing machine that was my grandmother Lessie's. It was an old Singer sewing machine with which I eventually made my own maternity clothes. For a time, sewing was something I really enjoyed doing and remember doing well. I received compliments on the clothes I made. There was also a special feeling attached to using my grandmother Lessie's sewing machine, just knowing it had belonged to her. It was a Singer portable foot-pedal model and it sat on a little table that had been part of a set of bedroom furniture. We kept it in the bedroom I shared with Faye. I learned to sew in Mrs. Vandenbosch's home economics class at Girls Poly.

Growing up I always knew my mom wanted what was best for us. Her way of doing so included taking us to all her club meetings and teas where we learned the ways of ladies and grown women. It was also important to my mother that we always be neat and presentable, no matter what. We were a reflection on her in the best sense of the word. My sister and I were encouraged to belong to a teen group called "Les Femmes." This club prepared young women for their social coming out or "debut." The debutante experience just felt foreign to me and I remember resisting it all even as I was participating. I never actually said, "No, Mom, I don't want to do this," but I never felt comfortable either. And I never actually "came out." I did not have that debutante presentation because I got pregnant. My sister, however, was presented as a debutante. I attended her ball and I remember what a big deal it was for my mom. I don't exactly remember my father being present. (He was.) Today I look back on those photographs with ambivalence. It was what it was. Joining "Les Femmes" was not something I wanted to do yet I almost couldn't get away from pressure to join in such organizations and their activities.

I could never voice my view to my mother or the other well-meaning and well-respected women of my community that I felt these clubs were elitist and exclusionary. It would have been far too painful for them and for me to hear those words out loud. In the 1980s, Freddye Petett of Delta Sigma Theta put my name in for membership and I declined to go forward. Freddye was then my boss at the Urban League of Portland and I liked and respected her enormously. Yet it didn't feel like me and I did not want to be identified with something elitist. I later got another invitation to join Alpha Kappa Alpha from Mrs. McClendon; her husband, Bill was one of my mentors and a revered figure in the Portland Black community. I declined. Just recently I was reminded of the costs of keeping my distance from the sororities. The National Organization of Black Women Lawmakers was recently in town for a conference. The focus was on diabetes education and the Deltas and Alpha Kappa Alpha's were major sponsors for the event. During the conference, their members were acknowledged with cheers and other signs of appreciation; there is a healthy competition that goes on between them that helps advance the good work they do. Yet there were a lot of women present who were not Deltas or AKAs. The sororities' "in-groupness" left these women out, and however inadvertently set up "the Other." I sat there at the conference thinking: "Here we go. It's 'Les Femmes' all over again."

It remains difficult to name what troubles me about these important and historic organizations. In Portland, it is said that the AKAs are darker-skinned African American women and the Deltas are women who are of lighter skin. Membership is also tied to income and marital status, as with the very well-to-do Jack and Jills Club. It is amazing how all of that hierarchy plays out in organizations that unquestionably do good in the community by fostering sisterhood and fellowship. Church women's groups or ministries in my experience are worlds apart from the club and sorority scene. Another whole segment of community can be found through the fraternal orders like the Eastern Star and Elks. Of these organizations, the clubs and sororities are tied up in class-based expectations about proper femininity and sexual-self presentation.

These pressures literally ate at me as a child and adolescent. I have a memory of having something of a nervous tic. I used to bite my upper lip in a way that would leave a mark on my skin. I did this in my years at Highland Grade School. I was conscious of the mark that my biting left but I have no memory of talking about it with anyone or of anyone in the family saying anything to me about it. It was a way for me to relieve pressure, it was a self-comforting measure. Something was literally eating me inside, being chewed away, and my habit made it visible on the outside. Yet no one noticed. It was a silent mark made by my mouth that no one could "read" on my skin.

It is ironic that recently I was reminded in public that I am thought of as someone who could not be prodded into speech. I just received an award at Vancouver Avenue Baptist Church and someone stood up to say as part of their congratulatory remarks: "You know, when she was part of our organization, we could never get her to say anything." I marvel at why and how this person thought a public award ceremony was the place to share this particular memory of me, with its suggestion of underperformance or deficit. I know that I am introspective. I reflect a lot before I speak and sometimes I don't speak. I heard the comment in that moment as a criticism and it felt like a criticism. The presenter also acknowledged a brilliant career, but I didn't internalize those words! Afterwards, another man, whom I'd only known slightly over the years, approached me and, after saying congratulations, underscored the earlier point: "Yeah, we never could get you to talk." What is a comment like this really about? I think it points to how a Black woman's speech is not her own; her voice can be coerced or silenced by just about everyone around her from family on out. Reclaiming my voice, my true, authentic voice—the right to speak or not speak as I see fit—has thus been a struggle, for even those closest to and most beloved by me have either not heard, not listened, or judged my silence pre-emptively. In the case of my chewed-up adolescent lip, no one could see or acknowledge the message I agonized to convey, that I literally had no words for.

During my chewed-lip years I remember not wanting to look at myself in the mirror because the mark was there. I have a vague memory of my sister asking about my lip. I know that I did not carry this tic into high school. In my memory, the tic is tied to having to constantly adjust to my father coming and going from the house and other strains. I know I felt some relief in my world when I started attending Girls Poly. By then I had girlfriends that I was pretty close to and we would walk to and from school together. That time felt free; just being out walking in our own world. I know my parents wanted "good girls"; the main definition of "good," however, was "obedient" and this equation proved disastrous when I was being sexually abused by my uncle.

It happened more than once and it always happened in the same place: my brother's empty room, a space already haunted by loss and violence. This uncle was my mother's youngest brother. He was not particularly liked by my dad, who thought that he was kind of a ne'er-do-well. Later in life he got involved with drugs and went to prison. When I worked in corrections, I actually saw him in prison. In our adult relationship, I never said, "Clarence, I forgive you." Forgiveness was unspoken for me. Back in time, whenever Clarence's name would come up in the family—usually disparaging his irresponsible behavior—I would defend him to his critics. Clarence did not threaten or physically coerce me. I think this is where the shame part of it comes in. I lived for years feeling like I had done something to deserve a punishment that never came. I felt complicit in something sinful or wrong. Even though I was just a little girl, I felt that somehow I had done something to bring on the abuse. Connected to the struggle with Clarence is a memory of a friend of my father's who used to come by the house when we were little girls. This man used to like to have my sister and me sit on his lap. I never felt comfortable doing that and always felt there was something not quite right about it. I spoke about it in the family but nothing

47

happened because he kept coming over and we were expected to be polite and not fuss. His behavior was "normalized" in our home. Looking back, I feel especially that silencing myself around my uncle's sexual abuse has shaped everything else in my life.

Just as abruptly as the abuse began, it ended. I think Clarence just went away around the time I started high school. I didn't tell anybody. It's possible that during the tortured silence of my molestation experience, I may have withdrawn further from communication with my mom. And despite the welcome change of Girls Poly, I brought the strain and confusion around my body with me. When I was fifteen or sixteen I tried to take my life with an overdose of aspirin. It happened in the bedroom that my sister and I shared. I remember a very painful period of just wanting to go away. I don't know if I became ill and then someone found me; I have no memory of exactly the sequence of events. My family knew something happened to me but they just didn't talk about "it." I do not remember if their concern involved taking me to a doctor. But I know about "after." My mom became more protective of me, not walking on eggshells exactly but wondering if I was all right and frequently asking if I was OK. I do not remember how I answered her questions but she had a way of looking at me with kind of a question mark. (Dad was the same way … asking if I was OK.) What I do remember is a cloud being there. And then the absence of a cloud as though people got silent. After the cloud lifted, from that point forward, I performed. I just performed and pretended that everything was OK. I kept going like that until things cracked and fell apart around 1980. But for a while, anyway, I became a different or new person.

CHAPTER FOUR

Them Changes

In my "new person" phase during high school, I had a boyfriend who lived almost literally around the corner (actually two corners). Neshell Waters was very popular. He was in a singing group called the Streetcorner Singers, and they had engagements all the time. He had worked for a short time at Fred Meyer; in fact, he was the first African American clerk to work at that store. This fact is important because he was not working in a janitorial role and his accomplishment was a huge thing back in those days. The NAACP had worked to make this happen. Neshell was also popular with girls. When we started dating he had a couple of other girlfriends, one of whom lived across the street! Like some of my girlfriends and their boyfriends, Neshell and I were sexual. We girls didn't talk about it a lot but one or two of us got pregnant before the end of high school. We did not practice birth control. In the class of 1965 at Girls Poly, I was one of roughly twenty African American students. My relationship with Neshell led to the birth of our son Tyrone Wayne Waters in 1966, named "Tyrone" for my brother and "Wayne" after Neshell's own middle name. We were married before our son's birth.

The only thing I remember about anticipating the world of adult sexuality is a book my mom gave me about menstruation and the changes in a woman's body. It was through reading that I made these discoveries. My knowledge of sexuality was not based on anything that she or my grandmothers sat down and told me. Sex was not really even a topic with my girlfriends. We would talk if we heard that someone got pregnant but there was no rite of passage or engaged conversation about how my body was going to change or how I or anyone else might feel about that. I still have a clear memory of the book being on the dining room table because my mom put it there and left it for me. My dad's way of talking to me about sexuality was a command: "Stay Away From Boys!" I don't

49

recall him saying: "Don't get pregnant." But we were not allowed to go to parties and I heard my dad's later objections to Faye going away to school at the University of Oregon as related to this issue of protection and control over our bodies. I also heard his objections to her wishes as somehow punishment for what I had done by getting pregnant. But my sister went away anyway. I think she and Mom just worked it out, thinking that Dad would catch up later. Grades were supposed to count for something at our house but I think it was hard for my father to think through support for his daughters' education, since school, especially college, seemed to entail freedom from home and distance from family.

Mom liked Neshell very much. She liked his family, especially his mom, who attended our church. When it was discovered that I was pregnant, the mothers were the ones who negotiated the marriage. Neshell and I married in August, and soon after that, he was drafted for service in Vietnam. We had lived in rental housing on North Alberta Street and then on North Going Street. Our marriage was not destined to last. We were very young and ill prepared for adult roles. After Neshell came back from Vietnam we separated and we stayed separated for well over a decade; we did not divorce until he decided to remarry. We always stayed in touch and maintained a good relationship around our son, and with our son, and for our son. I became very close to his second wife, Star. We were good friends and called ourselves the "wives-in-law." Other people could not figure us out but we really liked and respected each other. To this day, Star calls me every year on my birthday. We always acknowledge one another as women who loved and had a relationship with the same man

at different points in our lives. And our relationship was good for the kids.

Finding out I was pregnant was scary and I was afraid to tell my mom. In fact I couldn't tell my mom: she told me. She was the one who asked me if I was pregnant. I had to say yes because I was showing and she knew my cycle. But she did not shame me with a "How could you?" There was none of that. I was very afraid of what I was going to hear; the *What are the neighbors going to say?* tape was playing in my head. It was not a good time. Neshell's older sister, Doris, helped me get through. She knew I was pregnant and afraid and she just kind of embraced me and counseled me along: "Everything's going to be all right." To this day, she is Ty's favorite aunt. Though I was afraid to tell my sister I was pregnant, any memory of that conversation is completely blanked out by her joy at Ty's birth. She was just gloating and doting with happiness.

I finished high school and attended the graduation ceremony at Girls Poly. We all wore white robes and I was just beginning to show. Graduation was a really big deal as I was the first woman in the family to graduate. It was wonderful. My mom and dad and grandma were so proud. It was a real celebration and when I look at the picture taken of that day I can see satisfaction on my face. I don't know that I would say it was joy but nothing could really dim my accomplishment.

Graduation from high school led to a very challenging time for me. Neshell went off to Vietnam. My awareness of that war came through TV and, being a reader, I read about it in the newspapers, too. I have vivid memories of the "hot" wars of the "Cold War." I can still remember the Cuban missile crisis when the blockade was announced to the students at Girls Poly in the auditorium. I remember students crying; one student, Priscilla, had a brother in the service and I remember her tears. In terms of Neshell's service, I don't remember any preparation or other conversations about his absence. I do remember the presence of family. I had lots of family support and encouragement "not to worry." For the longest time, I kept a picture Neshell sent me of him sitting on a mound of bags during his tour of duty and he had a gun. That picture brought home to me that he was in a place of danger. He and I did not have much contact, like letters, while he was away. And when he came home, he was different. We were different. Whatever went on in Vietnam, Neshell was just locked up about it and did not discuss it. He remained a kind and generous man, extremely popular, and an exceptionally gifted singer.

After his return his old girlfriend, Star, entered the picture. They took up their relationship again. That was one of the reasons we separated. Neshell's war experience never became fully known to me, but I heard some details about a couple of people in his peer group, one in particular, who came back psychologically damaged. Folks knew that there was something terribly wrong with this man, as there was an incident where he actually had a gun and held his family hostage. The situation was resolved without anyone being hurt, but clearly that incident showed me how damaging war experience could be. As the years went on, I became more aware of this generation of men who had left the community to go serve and who came back tormented. They had stories but I only heard bits and pieces. Ty maintained a close relationship with his dad, and over time he got more of the story of what went on in Viet Nam. The fact that Ty's dad and uncle were in the service and wore a uniform in part led him to join the Navy and also wear a uniform.

After Neshell (he later changed his name to Sunni) and I split up, I was on my own—but not really on my own, because of family. My mom was always supportive and my sister was the same way, even while she was away at the University of Oregon. Sometimes I went back and forth to visit Faye in Eugene; sometimes she came home. Along the way I developed a desire to go back to school. In addition to my sister's enticing college career, I had a close girlfriend, Mildred Jones, who was already enrolled at Portland State University. She was having quite an experience and I wanted some of that. I wanted to increase my education. I was very aware that education was tied to the quality of life that I would be able to give Ty.

Mildred's friendship meant a great deal to me in my phone company days. She too was a reader. She invited me to visit Portland State University and I attended one or two classes with her. I remember being in an amphitheater style classroom and looking down at the professor. Being in a place of learning was exciting to me, as was seeing other Black students on campus. I had been working for Pacific Northwest Bell in the old 1900 Building for close to five years. With Mildred's example before me, I realized that I did not want to be there for the five-year pin and flowers. Some people at the company questioned my decision to leave such a good job with benefits. But the five-year pin (or the twenty-year pen!) just signaled to me something about small horizons even if I couldn't quite name it at the time. Something in my head said that if I stayed, I would be stuck. I also decided that I did not want *any* ceremony about leaving. I just wanted to go. Part of me had already deeply rejected that place. I remember well that when Martin Luther King, Jr., was murdered, not everybody at work was sorry that he had been killed. There is still heaviness around that tragedy for me. So by the time I determined to leave the company for higher education, I knew I did not want to celebrate with those people. I just wanted out.

At the same time, my family and friends had become even more invested in my success on the job. In that last year of work, I had been selected for a management-training program for testing computer technology. It was a big deal. People thought that wanting to leave was nuts, especially since I was leaving for the big question mark of higher education. But I was not looking at it that way at all. I was excited about coming to campus and joining Mildred and the other Black students. In retelling this passage today, my mind is drawn to the memory of a friend who asked me, in another workplace setting: "Is this job big enough for you?" It was my friend Norm Monroe. Even at that later time—more than a decade after I left the phone company—I was stunned by his words. I almost took them as an affront as I was then ensconced in highly valued work at the Urban League of Portland. I responded to promptings in myself about a "bigger" life by intuition, rather than out loud; that brought conflict. And, of course, I had been socialized in Portland, Oregon, where racism and sexism and paternalism tell Black women every day that we belong over *there,* away from choices and opportunities in life.

When I enrolled at Portland State. I had loans and grants, and worked part time. I had key-punch training, so I became a key-punch operator and worked downtown four to midnight while going to school. My mom took care of Ty and that's how I made ends meet. For a short time I was on welfare for the health care benefits and food stamps. It was embarrassing for me to collect benefits even though I had earned them and this experience and memory stuck with me when I entered the legislative and policy world.

My first year at Portland State was really significant because I met people who decisively influenced my thinking and life choices—for the next twenty years! I took courses in the Black Studies Department and was introduced to a literature that I was totally unfamiliar with and that I just thrived on. I was in a setting with Black professors; that experience was new. I had only had one Black teacher in my public school education. My poetry class with Primus St. John was transformational. I was keeping a journal and writing a great deal, including poetry. I was able to share my writing in this class and have my voice affirmed in a public way. I stood up and shared my poems with the class, and also one on one with Primus.

Receiving constructive critique was such an affirming experience, one of the first deeply affirming intellectual experiences I ever had in an educational setting.

By contrast I had an experience in Women's Studies at PSU that was very uncomfortable and negative. I took a course with Mildred and we did a project that involved interviews with a group of Black women in the community. We promised these women that we would share the information in the class—we played a tape recording of their stories—but that we would keep the tape in our own possession. The instructor insisted, however, that if we did not turn in the tape, it was going to affect our grade and that we would only get a C. We agreed to take the lower grade rather than break our promise to the women we interviewed. Here was a lesson about having Black women's words appropriated and our communal ethos violated, which Mildred and I successfully resisted.

Clearly, however, during my PSU years it hit me that my college choices meant leaving behind girlfriends from grade school and high school. As time went on I was not connected to them in the same way. We began living in different worlds, even though we occupied the same demographic space of the "Portland Black Community" or neighborhood. As I shifted my educational standing and employment prospects, white folks raised their own questions like: "Are you from here? You don't seem like you are from here." I'm never sure exactly what that *means*, but the effect is one of suspicion, alienation, and even rejection.

I was part of a group of PSU students who found each other and created community. Black Studies faculty communicated that we belonged on campus and in their classes affirmed that there was a place for us and for what we had to say. A few of us active Black students on campus had known each other from the community in North/Northeast Portland; a few of us had actually gone to Girls Polytechnic High School together. At PSU, we also formed study groups. I was focused on getting through successfully and worked at claiming and being claimed as a part of a community that tried to help other students get through. I also remember the encouragement of professors like Phil McLaurin, head of the Black Studies Department. Faculty also took the time to make sure that we had our financial aid packages together as well as any other support that we needed to do well on the campus. The Black students active in campus organizations created a comfortable place for ourselves.

Aside from that connection I was not tied into the general campus community life. If I wasn't in class I was working; if I wasn't working I was studying, and if I wasn't studying I was sleeping or taking care of Ty. Black students worked hard to create a sense of community but outside the space of our offices—Black Cultural Affairs and the Martin Luther King Jr. Scholarship Fund—we felt alien. The pride associated with this scholarship fund touched us on and off campus.

55

One year I received an award for my work on the fund and it was a welcome acknowledgement. There was a relationship between some of the pastors and organizations in the African American community and our campus groups. I was aware of organized, planned events, but I was not involved at that level of participation. One press conference involved Dennis Payne, who was an activist on campus who helped found the Black Studies Program, Rev. John Jackson, and a whole host of other community people.

During college I lived in a little one-bedroom apartment at NE Sacramento Street between what is now Martin Luther King, Jr., Boulevard and NE Seventh Avenue. The apartment complex was called Pru-Rey Gardens, and at the time, I was very conscious and proud of living in housing that was named after two black doctors, Dr. Pruitt and Dr. Reynolds. Dr. Reynolds was my father's doctor. I was aware of the significance of that history and by living there, I took strength from that history. The naming was significant to me. Yet I was also aware of the smallness of the actual living space; I wanted privacy and Ty needed privacy. We didn't quite have enough room and I had made the unwise choice of allowing my boyfriend Marvin to live with us—off and on. In these same years someone relayed to me that they had been asked if I was a hippie—not exactly an association I would make with the residents of Pru-Rey Gardens. Maybe Hawthorne Boulevard but not King Boulevard! I'd been wearing my hair natural since '67 or '68 and I wore jeans, but I was not quite sure where the "hippie" question was coming from. It was another case of feeling "Other." I knew I was looking for that place that would accept me for who I *am* not for what I do or look like. And at the same time, I was trying to figure it all out. Who am I? And what is my purpose? Instead of space for that question and its answer, I got more questions about my hair. "Are you going to keep your hair like that?" And "You know I really liked your hair better straight." These matters of personal style and femininity were key—and unresolved—since high school; it was like "Les Femmes" yet again, seventies style.

This situation could sting. One time some years later I was invited to a wedding in which the bride was a member of Delta Sigma Theta. The wedding took place at the World Forestry Center and it was a big deal. After the vows were said in the ceremony, there was a gathering of all the women in a circle. It was announced that all the women should come forward so they could sing a song to the bride. Upon hearing "all the women," I immediately stepped forward; then a woman whispered in my ear: "This is just for the Delta women." I felt that old sting of rejection. I also acknowledged that the moment epitomized what elitism behaves like—and I reject that behavior. I would never want to be the one whispering in someone else's ear: *you can't be a part of this.* It left me feeling odd or just left out. I chose to not participate or endorse certain modes of individual and collective expression. At the same time, I know that my lack of participation is related to not feeling good enough or "pretty" enough to join in, feelings of inadequacy tied to the script of racism and sexism inside me that played like old tapes.

My learning in Black Studies helped quiet some of these tapes. Extremely important to me was finding language to discuss taboo subjects like skin color and hair texture. In Black Studies these subjects actually came up in our classes! One professor asked us students: "Does skin color matter in the Black community?" and "How does that issue get talked about in the Black community?" I remember a huge discussion around skin color and my relief at being able to discuss color consciousness. I was able to make much clearer connections about assumptions I'd grown up with, like my mom's light skin and features and how she was always talked about as a beautiful woman. In Black Studies classes we analyzed how these judgments get played out in the community at large. So in an historical sense and also in a personal sense I connected historical references to darker-skinned women as being "less than" or part of a certain social class and women with lighter skin as part of another social class. I now understood that these judgments were tied to real status issues like club memberships and other social privileges. Black

Studies introduced language to frame questions about many things about race and power that I only silently observed while growing up.

My college education was driven by curiosity, a love of reading, and a real urgency about all there was to know! I was introduced to writers like Ralph Ellison and Zora Neale Hurston. Years later I would visit her hometown and a museum named for her in Eatonville, Florida. I was excited to find myself, so to speak, in the history of Black people on the pages of all those books we were assigned to read. I also experienced feelings of loss and anger like, "Why didn't I get this in high school?" And "How do I get caught up?" Mildred and I talked in those terms. As Black Studies students we were comfortable with the general idea of Black Power and we cheered for world-class athlete Tommie Smith when he raised his fist at the Mexico City Olympics in 1968. That was all "right on!" But my group of friends and I were also focused on getting through, doing well, and arriving on the other side, which for me meant being at home with Ty. At one point, I was also working from four to midnight, so I was often exhausted. Some of the activism, marches, and demonstration on campus remained on the periphery of my experience because I was extremely focused.

That said, we identified with the culture of the Black Power movement. We wore African-inspired clothing and jewelry. I had a big Afro pick with little designs on it. I had a leather jacket—not black but brown. Some of us went in for our naturals; those were our crowns. How the crowns looked was about how we looked and presented ourselves to the world. That was very important to me and Mildred. We put effort into our appearance, and for me, self-presentation was also about being ready to go to my job from school. I always carried a big bag or two with me for books; always something to write with, often my journal, and always something to read; *always.* Appearance was about being taken seriously on campus and representing our family and community. We knew we were downtown at the university and that we just couldn't show up unprepared.

CHAPTER FIVE

Operation Crossroads Africa

Black community connections at PSU included the African diaspora. Dr. Eno Ukage of Nigeria taught in Black Studies and presented to me the opportunity to participate with Operation Crossroads Africa, a premier student-exchange program founded in 1958 by Dr. James H. Robinson, an African American Christian minister. I applied for the program, was accepted, and even had women in the community, "Friends of Africa," raise funds on my behalf. I feel blessed to have had a mother who was so clear with me about it all: "You are going to take this trip." Ty was around five years old at the time, but she and my dad and my sister would make sure that Ty was OK. That was a gift.

My sojourn to west Africa turned out to be a life-changing experience. I participated with students from all over the United States, over a hundred total, and we were split into groups of about a dozen. The Crossroads program was in its way multicultural. Black and white students from different parts of the U.S. took part. We had our orientation at Rutgers University in New Jersey and going there was my first experience traveling alone, away from home. I had to present myself to "strangers in a strange land." Making this first journey east gave me the confidence to later return to search out my brother in New York.

An asset I brought with me to Crossroads Africa was my temperament as a quiet observer. I took it all in, kept my journal, and took pictures. I was one of the oldest members of our student group, by four or five years. Our student leaders were just a few years older than me. My age and life experience set me slightly apart, but I became friends with two or three people in the group, and I shared a lot at that level. There was a wonderful woman from New York named Sharmin Gray, whom I just loved. She had New York energy and a "meet the world!" kind of enthusiasm that was totally unselfconscious and infectious. I loved spending time with her and just being in her presence. There was another woman, I think she was from Mississippi, a white woman, and I was drawn to her amazing accent. It was a first time I had been in the presence of someone from the South who was white who really had the layered accent I associated with my own family and our Texas roots. I loved to listen to her speak because it was a form of music to me; that's how I heard her. And there was another young woman, Lisa, who was a student at Sarah Lawrence College and I was intrigued by her sense of entitlement to comfort, resources, and attention, all very much a product of her upper-class background.

I really got drawn into listening and learning everyone's story. Our group of ten students was made up of people from all over the country. We were mostly African American; there were three or four whites in the group. Interestingly I had less conflict with the white members of the group than some of my Black peers did. Because I had been raised in a white-majority community in Oregon, like Girls Poly, I was less ill at ease with white members of my group. At the same time, my socialization kept me kind of outside the group of Black students; I was aware of feeling outside their common experience of being socialized with more Black people. But as individuals I got to know them all. Ironically, in Africa I was able to get to know each of the students as individuals as opposed to being

representatives of a "group." I was conscious of the importance of this for me at the time: getting to know each person as an individual. The entire experience fired my curiosity about things unfamiliar; never before had I had such an adventure.

We spent most of our time in Nigeria, living in a village called Osi Okero not too far from Ile Ife, the historic cultural center of the country. Our job was to help the villagers build a maternity hospital from the ground up. We started with clearing the earth, we made mud bricks and laid those bricks, shoulder to shoulder with the people in the village. We lived in the chief's compound and experienced a totally different way of life than I had known in the

United States. We were engaged in village life and I allowed myself to experience a genuine immersion. The graciousness of the chief at Osi Okero and the women who were his wives stands out in my memory. They made us so comfortable. We were like extended family! We lived in a compound structure, largely made of concrete with a corrugated roof. The color I associate with our living space is golden yellow. It was shared space but segregated by sex. We had chores every day. At night, there would be a lot of conversation and sharing by candlelight or torchlight, sometimes indoors, sometimes outdoors. I remember sometimes trying to read or write by dim light. I also remember trips to the latrine, knowing that someone from the student group was probably going to pull a prank—and fearful of something worse from the forest around us! It was a little scary in the dark but also magical because of the absence of distracting artificial light. Against the night sky I felt so tiny, yet the stars felt so close to us, just at the horizon. It was magical.

The marketplaces were bustling with energy and people. The smells were rich and complicated; of foods but also of the limited sanitation and open sewers. Music was everywhere in open-air restaurants and other settings. All the bargaining in the market made an impression on me. It was like a game and it added excitement and human dimension to my American notions of shopping. At the marketplace people seemed especially alive, living life!

Day to day in Osi Okero, we had regular assigned tasks related to building the hospital. On the weekends, we would take bus trips to different places in Nigeria, to Ife, up to Ibaden, Benin, and to the Kainji Dam. At one point we teamed up with students at the University of Ife and we put on an event called "An Evening of Black Poetry from Africa and America." We put this event on at the United States Information Service's auditorium, with their sponsorship. The notice was published in the newspaper. On the evening of the event, all these people showed up—it was standing room only!— and I was completely taken aback. It felt magical, almost unreal, to be standing in Africa together with African and American students, presenting poetry from our two continents. I still have the reel to reel tape of the evening and the poster we made for publicity. It was quite an experience.

I only felt fear a couple of times in Africa, traveling at night. During our bus rides, we would arrive at various checkpoints. It was just after the Biafran War, so we ran into various "highwaymen" who expected payment for road passage. It came down to payoffs. Though in general we felt quite protected, sometimes

AN EVENING OF BLACK POETRY

FROM

AFRICA AND AMERICA

USIS AUDITORIUM, COCOA HOUSE, IBADAN
WEDNESDAY, AUGUST 4, 8:00 p.m.

ADMISSION FREE

our group leaders negotiated while the rest of us sat on the bus quaking. One time when we were stopped we heard music in the otherwise silent African night. As we strained to listen we realized that it was Buddy Miles (of Hendrix fame) playing "Them Changes." We all wondered, "What is Buddy Miles doing out here?!" And "From where out there in the dark is this coming? Someone's house?!" We struggled to put that music together with a picture, so we all invented the story that Miles must have been playing a "gig" out there somewhere. It was common for us Americans to hear James Brown blaring out from the market stalls and shops in the African cities we visited. In turn, we developed an ear for the sensational Fela Kuti, who just then exploded on to the music scene. I dance (and exercise!) to Fela's music today.

I still carry images from that trip that are crystal clear, like being able to look up at the night sky and feel like I could reach up and pull a star down. We visited a so-called zoo where the animals roamed freely; there weren't any walls anywhere! The villages were all laced with footpaths that seemed to fit and welcome my feet.

One member of our group became very immersed in African life and wanted a new name. There was a naming ceremony and he took the name "Segun." We made special preparation for the ceremony; we were given special clothing for the occasion. There was lots of drumming. Segun had taken the lead in organizing the poetry event at the USIS. Poetry and drumming and color are connected in my mind with memories of Africa. One excursion we made was to meet the Obas, who demonstrated the talking drum. The talking drum allowed messages to be sent some distance away and then acknowledged by drum in return. I remember Segun feeling very supported in his decision to change his name.

Our group certainly had its tensions and some were racial. A white woman student got involved with a male African student and it became a source of negative energy and gossip for some in our group, but mostly people had a "live and let live" attitude. Some students complained about the books available in the USIS library, as books by Black authors were conspicuous by their absence. I carry many images of children with me from that summer, some of whom were malnourished. I experienced some anxiety over the fact that we did not complete the hospital before we left. We got a great start, with the walls up (partially). I was acutely aware of "white elephant" projects all over Africa—somebody's do-good project or partial investment—that never got completed. I remain troubled about outsiders who go to Africa without ever completing their projects. What does that say about attitudes toward African people and their needs?

And at the end of the summer, we took a one-thousand-mile journey by bus with our student friends from the University of Ife up to Abidjan, Ivory Coast (we departed for the U.S. from the airport there). On that journey, as we traveled through the countries of Benin, Togo, and Ghana all along that magnificent coastline, we got to know each other even better. The close camaraderie of that journey was quite something. I deeply enjoyed living in the dorms at University of Ghana. There was a wonderful young man that I met at this time, named Leke. He was Nigerian. We spent a lot of time together that summer and we definitely had a crush on each other. I still have a picture of the two of us. I learned after we returned to the U.S. that he was killed but I still don't know how. Leke is a reminder to me about the fragility of life and the importance of all relationships, no matter how brief they might be. It was especially meaningful to see the university grounds again thirty-six years later, when I traveled to Ghana with my PSU Black Studies colleagues in 2007.

When I returned to the U.S. in the late summer of 1972, my sharpest memory is of seeing Angela Davis on the cover of *Newsweek*. I bought the magazine and still have it in my collection. Angela Davis had a big Afro and she had just been arrested. It was such a shock. I remember looking at that, thinking "Oh my goodness." It was like being rocked into another reality and I felt apprehensive.

I experienced a kind of culture shock going to Africa for the first time—then there was the shock of re-entering the United States. That re-entry was a time of depression. I remember sitting on my mom's porch for what seemed like hours just kind of in a daze. As I watched the cars go by in the neighborhood, I rethought all the things that had happened in Africa. I listened to peoples' conversation with changed ears. Everything just seemed so trivial. By contrast, living and working in Africa was an integrated experience. There, a meal meant going to the market place, working hand in hand with others to make the meal, and then sharing it collectively in the village. There was no refrigerator in the village to just get up and get a cold chicken leg on a whim. There was none of that! In fact we lost one of the members of our group who just had an emotional meltdown. He wasn't able to handle what some at the time called "deprivation." For example, we had no showers and no baths. Water had to be trucked in from the city and stored in big barrels. Some we used for cooking and the rest for washing and hygiene.

Back in the United States, the amount of stuff people had seemed like too much for me. It took me some time to really reconnect. Looking back I know that period marks the beginning of my disconnection from materialism. From then on, I became someone who did not need to have a lot of new things, like a new car. Some people have to have a new car every two years. Not me. I feel the same about money and income. I am content to have enough to take care of the basics but this matter of excess? I don't want to get caught up in having "stuff." Even when it was not explicit, my son always heard and appreciated my position on materialism. I try to take this stand in a way that does not judge other people. Books, art, music have been important to feed my spirit—also silence.

My experience in Africa was profoundly life altering in terms of values like materialism and consumerism. It also fired my desire to learn more about African history and culture. I remember writing a promise to myself in one of my journals, that one day I would be able to share what I know and travel back to Africa. I've been very intentional about keeping that promise through four trips to seventeen nations on the continent. While I was in Africa, I lost a lot of weight, even though my memory is of eating plenty of bread. When I returned people commented on my physical change as well as my emotional change. People said to me that I seemed different, even more pensive than usual. I've always been accused of being too serious!

When I returned to Portland State, I reconnected with my political science major. I was drawn to the subject matter out of curiosity, and it just seemed to fit me. Then I met Dr. Lee Brown who was the head of the department called "Law Enforcement." He encouraged me to take one of his courses and I did. Lee Brown alerted me to the fact that law enforcement was a field with emerging careers for women and people of color. He invited me to be a part of the cadre of people who would break through this largely segregated employment area. An additional incentive was the LEAP program, which would cover student loans for those who went to work in the field. I enjoyed Lee Brown's courses immensely because he challenged us to think critically, to write and express ourselves clearly, and to go out into the community and engage. Lee Brown also brought into our classroom wonderful speakers who embodied the best in the profession and he himself was very personally engaging—in addition to being a towering presence in the field, eventually Police Commissioner of Atlanta and then of the City of New York, the first African American to hold that position. I also studied with Dr. Gary Perlstein and he became another mentor. I just loved and admired them both; and to this day they remain my friends and people who have followed my progress.

REFERENCES
"Angela Davis Case." *Newsweek* v. 76 (October 26, 1970) p. 18-22.

CHAPTER SIX

The Correcting Influence

The sun was shining on the day I graduated from Portland State University. I have some beautiful photographs of the occasion— spectacular black and whites—in my family collection. The photographs show my mother and father, my son (of course), the person I was dating at the time, Marvin McKinley, my grandmother Alberta Louise Randolph, Mrs. Idella Burch (my sister Faye's mother-in-law), Faye's daughter Michelle, and some other friends. Faye herself was not present. She had cut short her education at the University of Oregon just shy of graduating, due to her own family pressures. On my graduation day, she was at work. Nonetheless it is a warm memory. Marvin's friend Walter was the photographer. The pictures show pride in the eyes of my mom and dad and grandmother and Mrs. Burch. It was an extraordinary day, as I was the first person in the family to graduate from college. It was historic for another reason; it was the day Richard Nixon resigned, August 8, 1974. I had watched the Watergate hearings all summer and was aware of Barbara Jordan's role. Her magnificent voice just captured me, as it captured the whole nation. During graduation, televisions were on in Smith Center and people were caught up in that moment as well. I stepped into Smith to take a look. And then the very next day, I went to work with the State of Oregon Corrections Division as a counselor in a work release facility for women.

Despite being on track with a new job, during my college years I had got lost somehow. I have a strong memory of my mother saying to me that she felt that I was changing and that this change threatened to disconnect our relationship. While studying at PSU I also experienced bouts of depression and I would isolate myself from friends and family in order to cope. I would just kind of disappear. I was living on my own and I needed a quality of emotional support that I did not know how to ask for. My mother seemed critical of me and had her own frustration around not being able to communicate with me. I think we both sensed that the changes I was making could take me even further from the reach of family. That frightened both of us in different ways.

My peers and friends faced employment and family pressures similar to my sister Faye's and mine. Mildred wanted to participate in Operation Crossroads Africa but had not been able to get the finances together. That was painful because we had hoped to do that program together. I had been able to get a scholarship. I also got support from the women's club community as well as another organization of women in higher education. Mildred did not have the same combination of support. I felt hurt for Mildred, my best girlfriend, and even guilty that I was going to Africa anyway. Happily, when I went to New York to find Tyrone, the two of us went together.

The material I encountered in Lee Brown's classes aided me enormously as I moved from college to the world of work again. One telling assignment in an administration of justice class concerned police-community relations. The students were supposed to write an essay about "Officer Friendly," but I maintained that the typical police officer was experienced as something quite other than "friendly" in the Black community. I brought that awareness into the classroom. In these years I was aware of the Black Panther Party in Portland, especially their free breakfast program and free clinic, though I was not personally involved. I also remember at that time that some people in the African American community were afraid of the young folk who identified with the Panther Party. Anger was certainly felt and expressed when Fred Hampton was murdered by police in Chicago and after police-related incidents in Portland. These events put people on edge and some of that concern carried over into the classroom.

Lee Brown's classes allowed me to make clear and urgent connections between my learning and community life. Plus Dr. Brown was someone who extended himself beyond his department to support students. He encouraged me to apply for a Police Foundation program in Washington, D.C., and later for an internship with the Portland Police Bureau—a paid internship. My work with the Police Bureau involved conducting a study of police overtime practices. In the early 1970s, there was concern about the number of hours police officers spent at the county courthouse, waiting to be called to testify, as well as about overtime practices in general. My work involved poring through files, records, and documents of officers' time spent in court. I performed very detailed, intense work by hand, not just tabulations but tracking and correlating figures for specific officers and specific shifts. By the end of my work, I was aware that someone in the Bureau was not happy about this study, as its findings could have an impact on officers' pay. It was very political.

My internship took place in the Planning and Research Department. The head of that department committed suicide during the time of my internship. It was just horrible. In addition, I made some unexpected discoveries in the police files. I came across a series of photographs; a lot of the photographs were of Black people taken in different circumstances in the community. Some scenes looked like clubs or parties in peoples' homes; the images suggested that the photographer had to be very close to the participants to take the shot. It made me think: "informant." I wondered about who took the pictures and about who was close enough to such settings to do so. Then I got scared. I needed to tell somebody—but not at the Bureau. I shared the information with Ronnie Herndon. He told me to be careful.

My Police Bureau internship supervisor was Sergeant Schwartz. We attended the Washington, D.C., Police Foundation conference together. When we returned to Portland, he became my supervisor at Planning and Research. Our office was in the Fourth Avenue Building, which was being remodeled and was in a bit of a jumbled physical state. One day, Sergeant Schwartz asked me to vacuum the office. I had to tell him that that was not going to happen. Another time, he wanted me to go pick up a pair of shoes of his at the store. Again, I had to tell him "No, that's not happening either." I remember there was a thing around coffee and who was going to make it. Sergeant

Schwartz placed really sexist expectations on me. I shared these experiences with girlfriends at the time, which helped me put it in perspective; on the job I just tried to concentrate on getting the work done. My findings showed that certain officers had a pattern of getting the most overtime. In the end, someone actually challenged one of my graphs, but there was so much other data that my findings stood.

Despite my unnerving experience at the Police Bureau Dr. Brown and Dr. Perlstein guided me to local job opportunities in the field of law enforcement. My job in Oregon Corrections came to me through Dr. Perlstein, one of the other people at PSU who had let me know that my voice mattered, that my voice counted. He let me know early on in my career as a student that he appreciated my critical thinking skills and ability. Shortly after I graduated, we served on a corrections-based committee and I ended up voting "no" on some contentious matter before the group. I remember him expressing pride to me that I was able to stand by my principles in a room full of people where I could have easily been intimidated into just going along with the majority. Dr. Perlstein had told me about employment openings in the corrections division and encouraged me to apply for a position. Dr. Brown provided me with a reference. Were it not for their mentoring, I probably would not have changed my major to Administration of Justice and gone in that career direction.

I wasn't interested in police work on the street, so to speak, but more interested in corrections and the community side. The day after graduation from PSU, I had a job waiting and I went to work in the State Corrections Division. I was a counselor in a work-release facility for women coming out of prison in the Portland Women's Center, located in Northwest Portland. Part of my job involved traveling to the women's prison and interviewing women for the program for education and work release. I quickly sized up the racist bias of the screening process since most of the Black women wound up on work release and the white women wound up on education release. Work release was far more punitive. Being unemployed thirty days after release resulted in the client's remand back to the institution. Calling this bias racism was my first experience of taking on the system in the interest of equity. It was also my first experience with pushback from those who preferred the status quo and who questioned the legitimacy of my criticism. I heard things like: "What are you doing?" and "Nobody else has raised this so what's the big deal?"

To meet these challenges, I got community people involved. I assembled an advisory board for the program with members representing the different kinds of services that women needed to transition back to community. These included the faith and social services communities. One of the key things I learned from Lee Brown's classes—he was known as the "Father of Community Policing"—was that if female former convicts were going to be successful in reconnecting to the community, supports had to be in place. Support was essential prior to their arrival and the advisory board was one way that we started to make change and pave the way for them. That was great, ground-breaking work and I enjoyed it immensely.

Yet I was working in a system in which you could count on one hand the number of Black people—or any people of color—working in the field. I had written a paper on locating transitional programs in communities in order to make them a win for everybody (these were also days of "Not in My Backyard"). I was very proud of this paper; it had gotten an "A." I had the book learning but I also knew my community very well. I knew precisely how to put these things together. I had a supervisor named Manfred Moss who, as part of the interview for the job, expressed interested in anything I wrote. He saw the paper, liked the paper, used the paper for his own benefit. Having my work appropriated was a searing learning experience. I now realized that I had to pay careful attention to what I knew and exactly how I shared it at the workplace. I needed to convey authority without ceding that same authority to others. Don't let anyone diminish what you bring to the table—or steal it either—was the lesson I learned, an update on my Women's Studies experience.

At Oregon Corrections I was an oddity. And challenging the system made me a target. I was quickly labeled a troublemaker yet I was insistent about change. Corrections staff also manifested other kinds of racism, and openly made slurs, like referring to clients as "another nigger in the wood pile," a disparaging reference that comes straight out of slavery. It was just crazy, crazy, crazy.

After a time, I became acting manager of my women's program. But by the time the selection process for a new director came up my interest had shifted to parole and probation. I applied and got an appointment at the East Portland office on Northeast Glisan Street. When I showed up for work the first day, the supervisor acted like he didn't know that I was coming. He did not have an office ready for me. They created a little cubbyhole place out in the hallway that was not really an office. I declared, "This isn't going to work." Unlike the Portland Women's Center, where I was totally isolated, there was another quietly supportive Black man in this new office. I also had a remarkable white ally named Mike McGee, who held my hand and walked me through this predominantly white male minefield. Mike had been one of the participants in Freedom Summer in Mississippi and had some consciousness about how racism worked.

We wrestled the thing out around proper office space until I got one. Then there was the matter of caseload. I wanted a mixed caseload because that's what everybody else had. They wanted me to have an all-female caseload and I resisted. Then they wanted me to have all Black folks. I resisted that, too. To me, these practices smacked of Jim Crow and segregation and were unacceptable. At the same time, my observations of how clients were treated started to accumulate. Black clients faced things that were outrageously racist and just wrong. They were spoken to like animals, in derogatory and demeaning racist terms. I had to call that stuff out in a setting with people who had never had a life experience working professionally with a Black person or any people of color. My head just screamed: *What is this, a plantation?! The KKK?! What have I walked into?!*

I was in extremely hostile territory but I worked hard to establish who I was and my own solid reputation with clients as a fair person.

Black clients especially tended to see counselors as part of the system and "the man." I wrote a series of memos to the head of corrections to document what was going on. My emphasis was on training—back then it was called cultural sensitivity or awareness— to deal with race and racism. I also pointed out the need to deal with gender issues. I even named Dr. Darrell Millner of the Black Studies Department as a resource. I was not complaining. I identified problems and the resources to deal with those problems. I also thought that, if I wrote it down, somebody would have to pay attention. Perhaps in my mind it was also a form of protection; somebody else had to know other than the people in the office who were giving me the blues. But when my supervisor found out that I had sent the memos, I was targeted as a troublemaker. Nonetheless I got a response from above. A shake-up was going on and it had to do with how I was being treated by the supervisor at the Glisan office. They pegged me as a troublemaker, but at the same time, someone higher up agreed some training needed to be put in place.

I wound up being transferred to another office in North Portland. The issues there were the same. But this time it was an all-white-male environment—no other Black staff, no Mike McGee—and I started to feel very afraid in that setting. My caseload was manipulated to put me in what I felt were unduly dangerous situations, like a home visit to former motorcycle gang members without adequate support and cover. I gave voice to my fear on the job and they exploited it. Another white male employee stalked me. He had an apartment one block from where I lived and he would come by my place and leave me notes, "just" letting me know that he was around ... somewhere. I took my issues to the union but they did nothing. I felt totally unprotected. I told people in my community about what was going on and asked them to check on me if I did not come home from work at night. The work really wore me down over time.

I had some clients that I knew, or knew my family, especially some of the Black women. Others I knew through the experience of the Portland Women's Center. I always tried to be fair and to show that I cared. For example, if I was driving down King Boulevard (then Union Avenue) and saw a woman from my caseload standing on a street corner, I would not do the drama stuff and call for another probation office to come with handcuffs. I would get out of my car, talk to her, and remind her where she had been (jail), talk about the kids (if there were kids involved), and run the whole thing down. Many of the women I met were smart. But they had done dumb things, usually with some dumb guy. A woman who now attends my church almost died of a heroin overdose. She also engaged in prostitution and sold drugs, but that is a closed chapter in her life. She uses that experience in her life as a teaching tool or testimony with younger women. When we see each other, there is a reverence in our relationship that is about an understanding of grace that we have each experienced in our lives. She knows my story and I know hers. There is no judgment in it. I met and counseled a white woman who shot her husband after he abused her for years; she lost her children. I will never, ever forget the grief I saw in her eyes.

In addition to working hard to overcome the mistrust of clients I had another role as the organization's correcting influence, a role that was unpaid and unwelcome but utterly necessary. I became the voice for justice and for correcting things that were wrong, just wrong. For four years, I did that work in corrections, including the years when I transferred to parole and probation. I had to invent a way to be in order to do my work with integrity—and also to stay sane. Over and over again, I had to work with people who didn't know what they didn't know about their narrow range of life experiences and their own racism. It made the work extremely difficult. It took a serious toll on me. I always experienced the stress of being "the only one"— meaning the only Black person—with all eyes watching everything I did, anticipating a mistake. Every day I worked with people whose only frame of reference for race relations was the Black folks that they saw on TV or whom they saw in some subordinate position like maid, servant, slave, or, most pointedly, criminal.

I had no real outlet for the pressure this situation created for me. There was no support internally at all for examining institutionalized racism in corrections. Educationally, I had been well prepared to engage these very issues. I knew the language. I also had a good employment record and saw myself as someone experienced in working with a lot of different people. I was not prepared for lack of any kind of support on the job. I also was not prepared for the emotional and psychological toll that mounted as I essentially took on two jobs: "the work" and then "the correcting influence."

At the time, I held a lot of my experience close, just held it in. When I finally decided to leave corrections after over four years, I ran into a gentleman, Mr. George Rankins, who was director of the Urban League Employment Program in town. He let me know in his way that he was disappointed that I had left the state corrections division because it's so hard for Black people to land those jobs. I remember really feeling the weight of his words. He let me know that I had let down the race without exactly saying, "You let down the race." The way he spoke inflicted something into my spirit. He had no idea of what I had gone through. I couldn't find a voice, literally, to even say what all had occurred and what I had seen. I don't know that I did respond to him at all. I did not really have the words to say where I was or describe what I had endured. I just did not have it.

What I did have in me were memories of how racism worked in my life. My experience in corrections put me in a place of remembering growing up on North Williams Avenue and how we kids used to keep this little pile of rocks in the front yard for the white people who would drive by and call us "nigger" while we were outside playing. We would just chuck a rock. The white men in parole and probation also had violence on their minds. They were mostly men who wanted to be police officers but hadn't made that grade. A number of them wanted to be armed—as probation officers! It was a dangerous group of people with a dangerous mentality. By words expressed and unexpressed in their treatment of Black clients, they were dangerous.

I had to get out of there so I quit. And I went home to heal. It took me a good six months or so just to start feeling like a human being again, like I was getting back to me. I had compartmentalized the strain and told myself: "I can handle this." I did not tell any family members about it. My father's way with me and my sister, until the day he died, was: "If anyone is ever bothering you, be sure to tell me about it." And what he meant was: he had a gun! Was it registered? No! So I wasn't going to tell him about it. A lot of it was bluster, but he also meant it. Long after, I shared some of these experiences with others and they asked why I didn't sue for harassment or discrimination. But I wasn't thinking like that. Today, I'm very good figuring that stuff out and knowing how to act on it. My challenge then and now was that I take the racist push back in the heart and the emotional part of it starts to take its toll. The toll becomes so heavy that I can't even speak about it. The harm and woundings have a silencing effect. Part of me imagines a place where I'm supposed to figure this all out, but it is by myself. Speaking out loud becomes very, very difficult.

A complicating factor in my years in corrections was my relationship with Marvin McKinley, who was also a student at PSU. It was a hot and heavy relationship for a while, but it had a really bad ending. Today we would call it domestic violence. At one point he actually held a live gun to my head and threatened to kill me. He also raped me. It was an emotionally and physically abusive relationship. It was horrible and had a horrible ending. The situation traumatized me in ways that I wasn't even aware of for many years, many years. Things got so bad that I finally told my father and my brother what was going on. The two of them confronted Marvin and I believe threatened him with his life in order to make him stop.

I married Richard Mayfield in August of 1979. Rev. John Jackson, pastor of our family's church, Mt. Olivet Baptist, performed the ceremony in my mom and dad's living room. Years later I said to Rev. Jackson about that wedding, "That was a terrible idea." And he said, "Oh, you thought so too!" And I said, "Well, why didn't you tell me!" He laughed in a way that told me he was in my corner. But back then I made poor choices that came out of low self-esteem. Richard was a former drug abuser and during our marriage he started up using again. I found evidence of his use around the house. When money started to disappear from the checking account, that confirmed what was going on to me. I was on the rebound from Marvin. Marvin had been someone very much around family yet my mom—not because I told her—seemed aware that things were not what they should be in the relationship. When the time came when I felt like I had to tell somebody about how bad it was, I told my brother and my dad. Later, Marvin moved to Seattle, where my brother Tyrone was living. Marvin and my brother had become friends. It appeared that way to me. I never quite understood how that happened and I had some anger—or angst—about it. I never spoke about my feelings, I just wondered how it was that they could have this relationship. Once I even saw Marvin in Seattle, at my brother's house. We managed to make amends. We closed a chapter in our lives and acknowledged that we had become different people, hopefully better people, and now we could go on.

That kind of closure never happened with Richard. I came to a point in that relationship where I realized that he was probably going to die of an overdose. And that is exactly what happened. After we had been separated for a few years I got a call that he had been found in the street. Whoever he was with when he OD'ed had just left him there dead, making me a widow.

I never really wanted to marry Richard. In my mind, we were not heading towards marriage. After we married and the emotional abuse escalated, I needed to extricate myself from the horrible, terrible mistake. There was a lot of shame around it for me. I was also concerned for Ty due to the things that he was witnessing and just sensing with his teenager's awareness that things were not right.

Years earlier, when Sunni and I tried to get back together after he returned from Vietnam, it was pretty public that the marriage was not working out. Our families were both members of Mt. Olivet Baptist church, my grandmother's church, so the church knew, through our moms. Our peers knew as well. I can still remember the joy and excitement of his mom as we showed her our rings standing in her kitchen. At some point I just stopped wearing the ring. I have a clearer memory of stopping wearing a ring after Richard and I split up. I still have the rings and lately I've been thinking about getting them melted down and turned into something else.

After Sunni, my social identity was predominantly "single mom." My first marriage was really about our parents' expectations that the two children who got in trouble would get married. There was not a whole lot of thought and preparation about marriage and what all of that meant. The second time, with Richard, my head was telling me: "I think I ought to be married by now." Some of my other friends were getting married. I don't think I married for safety or security, just a social expectation that I should be married. Yet at the very moment that Rev. Jackson had Richard and me repeat our vows, I thought: *why am I doing this?* He was a drug counselor when I met him. He had cleaned up years before and was working as a drug counselor at an organization called Comprehensive Options for Drug Abuse. He was also working on a counseling degree.

Yet from the day that the vows were spoken, it just wasn't going to work. I started seeing a therapist because things began by falling totally apart. Through therapy I realized I that I had to get out of the relationship. Therapy helped because when I accused Richard of using again, he denied it and called me crazy, even though I saw money missing from the checking account. That marriage involved the worst years of my life. Excruciating years. I experienced a lot of self doubt and deep, deep, deep depression to the point of contemplating suicide. I even checked myself in for a couple of weeks to the Providence psychiatric unit.

I was not able to tell anybody what was really going on with me in part because of shame. My mom had an awareness that something was going on; she tried to get through to me and talk to me but I just could not connect with her. During my hospitalization I started to wonder how being molested in my childhood had contributed to where I was and how my life experiences of physical and sexual violence were all connected. I'm still dealing with issues around self-esteem, worthiness, and shame rooted, I believe, in the experience of being molested by a family member. It was a really dark, dark passage. In 1980, the year that Mt. St. Helens blew its top, so did I.

The care I received at Providence was terrible—but I would like to acknowledge that Providence has greatly improved its delivery of services since that time to become a more culturally competent provider of mental health services. What I remember about that time was the silence, or rather, the silencing of my voice. I was unable to speak. I was not made to feel comfortable or safe. I was in a room by myself for part of the time. I remember a cross on the wall. There were counselors, therapists, and professional people around trying to get me to participate in a group. I was acutely conscious that everyone was white. But I checked myself into the hospital because I couldn't function. At one point in my hospitalization, I collapsed on the floor of the bathroom. I found out later that I had been given the wrong medication. The matter was never named or dealt with, much less resolved. My poor treatment became part of the trauma of it all.

For years afterward, every time I passed by or visited Providence Hospital, I was reminded of what I had experienced. In my head I would say: "One of these days I am going to be able to tell that story." I promised myself: "I'll get to a place where I can tell that story." I don't really know how I patched myself back together again, but I did. But I've been able to tell that story only as of this year. My experience has informed how I look at the mental health needs of others, all others. It turned me into an advocate around mental health issues, especially for African Americans, but it is really about the mental health needs of all people.

I would like to acknowledge the honor received from Providence Health and Services in 2008, an award that reads: *Providence Health and Services is honored to recognize the efforts of Senator Avel Gordly, whose compassion and wisdom have served to improve the lives of so many in our community.*

79

CHAPTER SEVEN

"She Who Learns, Teaches"

—African Proverb

During my marriage to Richard, I had accepted, in 1979, a position working as a case manager at the Urban League Senior Service Center. That opportunity came through a call from my friend Norm Monroe, who urged me to apply and who later encouraged me to apply for Director of the League's Northeast Youth Service Center. My years at the Urban League of Portland were good, rich years in my life. I learned much about the meaning of community that I put directly to work. I was deeply involved in the African American community through the program that we built at the Urban League. We focused on claiming our young people in a way that would keep them from having contact with the juvenile justice system, and for those who had already had that contact, we reclaimed them. We helped those young people and their family members to get information and alternatives to prevent further penetration into the juvenile justice system.

It was important to the success of this program for our counselors to be in the schools. We were one of the first Youth Service Centers in Portland. There were five Youth Service Centers in the city at that time and the Northeast Youth Service Center was administered by the Urban League. Our initiative was unique; since our counselors were located in the schools, they could have immediate contact with students who were identified as being at risk. By being on site, our counselors also had a link back to parents and other resources in the community. The program was all about being where kids were, being available to parents, and being both preventative and interventionist.

Our program succeeded in getting Multnomah County funding under the rubric of culturally specific services to citizens. This money in the early 1980s represented the first time that an African American community-based organization gained a significant amount of funding from the county—or from any funding source—to deal specifically with the needs of African American youth and families. It was a coup at the time, especially since there were other established organizations around, like the Morrison Center, who claimed to be serving the needs of so-called minority youth. We made another argument: in order to really make inroads with youth exhibiting negative behavior, they needed to be connected with people who looked like them; skilled, trained people who were part of their neighborhood and community. This funding allowed us to move the Urban League Youth Service Center program forward. And I'm very proud that we were able to do that work so successfully.

Our counseling program was full of stars. We had Jasper Ormond, one of the very few African American clinical psychologists to ever work in the state of Oregon. Now he's based in Washington, D.C., and doing wonderful work internationally. We had James Mason, who later achieved a Ph.D. and went on to manage the state Office of Multicultural Health in Oregon. Ben Priestley was a counselor very active in the Black United Front. Ben edited and published the national publication of that organization, the *Front Page*, and went on to groundbreaking work with the Housing Authority of Portland. Now retired, he has written a book with several other men of his generation about living with cancer. At the time, we knew that we had something special going on; that something special was a heart for service. We had love for community and a love for our people, Black people. We also believed that all people of good will could make something positive happen for young people who were struggling in school. Putting that team together was an important phase in honing my ability to recognize talent, pull that talent together, and then find ways to unleash our collective gifts in the community for good. Years later I returned to the Urban League to serve on the board; that service was an energizing and very affirming experience as well.

To accomplish the funding piece with Multnomah County we used the collective thinking of everyone at the Urban League. We had great writers on staff. One in particular was Renee Watson-

Taylor. Renee is today a member of my church, Highland Christian Center, where she also plays an administrative role, continuing her service to community. We came together in retreats—some at my house—where we could strategize together. We always considered how best to serve families and insisted that we couldn't separate the youth from their family unit. Moreover, the mainstream notion of the nuclear family unit didn't acknowledge that, within the African American community, extended family and even other people not blood kin were attached to a child and had to be factored into services. A lot of our work involved reframing "the problem," so to speak, and imagining the opportunities that flowed from that reframing. So while we were the "Youth" Service Center, we successfully made the point that we served families. Youth were not independent from whatever was going on in the family unit. We had collective genius; really smart people working together. This was a very talented, focused, and service-oriented group of people whose thinking was in alignment with the Urban League mission. When I look back, it was magical. When we received the two hundred thousand dollars from Multnomah County we were so elated you would have thought it was millions! Direct funding to African Americans for culturally specific services was political and there were those who hoped we would fail.

I think what allowed us to be heard and understood by entities like the Multnomah County Commission was that our Youth Service Center was part of the Urban League of Portland. The Urban League brought with it an identifiable history; people who were revered in the community were connected to it. When the Youth Service Center was in the room, it was the Urban League Youth Service Center. The name meant community. It was a time when some folks attached to that history, who were still living, could be called on strategically to help make our case. One of these elders was Otto Rutherford of the NAACP; he had worked for the passage of the 1953 public accommodations law. I met him on my first job with the Urban League, which was case manager at their Senior Center. At the Senior Center, where he served as director, I met him and other elders who were part of that movement in that era. At the time, I was not fully conscious about who some of the people were. I was trying to learn my new job! I was this young thing, and needed to be respectful and listen a lot. I sat at the feet of those who knew a whole lot more than I did and who had lived their lives fully. It was a rich opportunity to learn.

I was a college graduate and "trained" in that sense. I also had a family history in the community and folks knew my grandmother. As soon as they found out that I was Alberta Randolph's granddaughter or "Bea's daughter," or that Dad was a railroad man, that opened up all kinds of windows and doors with the elders. They knew about my mom and her connection to Eastern Star (she was a Grand Worthy Matron of the order). That these elders knew the family history paved some of the way for me to do the work of service as a case manager. At the same time, I was also working with elders who in some cases had little formal education, so sometimes we would kind of bump heads, especially when it came to paperwork. Case management documentation requirements affected funding. That requirement was a rub between us. I learned that my background and training were different—not better, but different—from those of the elders. In some cases, what my elders knew was better! Especially the value they placed on relationships.

We ran a telephone reassurance service, where volunteers and staff people called elders who were homebound to make sure that they were OK. We connected people to Meals on Wheels. We tracked foot care and diabetes. But it was the youth program that initially attracted me to the Urban League. Lolenzo Poe directed the Youth Service Center when I came on board; then as he left that position, I took it on. Both programs were based in the Martin Luther King Jr. Neighborhood Facility, adjacent to King School, so I didn't have to change physical locations when I changed jobs.

A number of people stand out from the King facility in the years 1979-1983, like the late Rev. Ira Mumford. He was a singer—in fact he had been part of a famous singing group—and he was always telling all of us outrageous jokes. He just had a way of making you laugh that allowed you not to take yourself too seriously. At the same time he was very much a man of the community, a man of faith. He was an elder at Allen Temple CME Church, a church I also attended from time to time. I saw him nearly every day and he was an inspiration. The King facility in general was a place young people could come to and find out where and how they might connect to other resources in the community. We wanted them to know that they had an advocate; not only the kids but their parents, too. We wanted to be a beacon of hope, and we were. Our days were full of voices and laughter and excitement and affirmations and often difficult situations. We counselors tried to be conscious of our own behavior; we were always modeling to the young people.

One time, I got in touch with Maurice Lucas, of the Portland Trailblazers. Maurice had a heart for service and when he wasn't dribbling a basketball he was always, always doing something meaningful out in the community. He came and talked to our kids and he always had a message about being your best self. We brought in people like Jawanza Kunjufu, out of Chicago, who was an educator, scholar, writer, and publisher. He did a lot of work around Black boys in the educational setting, especially around sexuality and race. Kunjufu analyzed the ways in which fear becomes a factor in the classroom when Black boys get older and bigger, and some teachers (especially white women) misinterpret certain behaviors. We brought

Shirley Chisholm visited Portland around 1982 at the behest of Delta Sigma Theta sorority. I received an honor from the Deltas at this event. Ty is pictured between us.

some of the best and brightest minds in the country to our center to get the best training and be that beacon of hope in the community.

I did both counseling and administration. I had a dedicated executive assistant and lots of volunteers. We believed in recruiting volunteers to help us with the work for several reasons. First, to help with the 8 a.m. to 5 p.m. work shift and then also to extend our availability after hours. A whole lot happens from 5 p.m. until the next day! And second, volunteering fostered new skills in the parents, grandparents, and other interested helpers who came to the facility. We met with school principals to make sure they understood our program of intervention and prevention. We offered ourselves as a point of contact for early behavioral issues among African American students. We let them know that we had access to parents, access to churches, and all kinds of resources. We were very hands-on.

Politically, I was also hands-on. In the funding process, it was my voice and that of the president and CEO of the Urban League, Freddye Petett, in the lead. Jasper Ormond also played a role. He was crucial in making the case for the culturally specific approach and its legitimacy. I was the person leading the center; I was the person who corralled all the right folks to assist in the process. Our opposition was never direct. At the regular meetings of the city's Youth Service Center organizations, some of the politics and questioning got played out. After my tenure, the county changed its way of delivering services to youth and the YSC that we created went away. Before that happened we started talking about going independent of the YSC system. Eventually, the program broadened and my job shifted from director of the Youth Service Center to the director of Youth Services in general for the Urban League.

At the same time, I was in this marriage that was going to fail, and I knew it. The marriage was coming apart and I was just barely holding it together. There was a deadline on a grant that I was having difficulty with; we were going to miss it. I was having panic attacks. The stress was coming out in physical form. I was not managing well and I was not speaking about it. My sister had some awareness that I was struggling but I don't even recall talking to her directly about what was going on. One day I had a panic attack that was so bad I wound up going to Kaiser Hospital from work. One of my staff came to the hospital. Her name was Hazel Polk. She let me know that if there was anything at all that she could do that she wanted to be of assistance. Hazel was a very spiritual, prayerful person. That visit to Kaiser was definitely a signal that it was just all coming apart. So I had a conversation with Freddye about it. Despite her offer of support I just could not pull it together. Around this time we had a Youth Service Center staff retreat at the coast during which some things happened that indicated that my tenure with the Urban League was over. It just wasn't going to work out.

Being fired was a relief. My burdens were too heavy, as was the mask I wore about it all. At this point in my life, I had still not fully disclosed to anyone how much pain I was in or that I was dealing with depression and the ghosts of having been molested. The end of my second marriage seemed to bring up all this stuff and I didn't have a place to deal with it. I went into counseling and each time we were only able to go so far. Race was a major barrier to deeper understanding and safety in therapy. The available therapists were all white and insensitive to cultural issues. What I owned was that I was dealing with a lot of shame and stigma. Also fear that "someone's going to find out how terrible I am" or find out that I was "really" incompetent. "What were my gifts, really?" A tape of self-doubt was rolling in my head.

Then a really wonderful thing happened. Jasper Ormond—who remains a friend to this day—pulled together a group of people and they came to my house to say: "We're concerned about you. And you're carrying too much. What can we do to help?" I remember that gesture of love and kindness with deep appreciation. This gesture and others that came once the news got out that I was no longer at the Urban League reminded me that people were kind and understanding. This passage also taught me the importance of asking for help. People around me recognized that I'd been struggling with something and they did not blame me for being fired or for "failing."

It was during this time that Jasper hit me with the question: "What is your purpose?" That question was like a lightening bolt.

The question raised other questions and, finally, a space for me to answer them. What am I doing? Who am I? What are my skills? What is it that I do? Who am I, really? How do I want to be appreciated, not for what I do, but for who I am? I needed help to figure that all out. I recall an ongoing issue between my father and me. When he acknowledged pride in the things that I did in the community, it pointed him to pride in the family name: Gordly. I had a hard time accepting his praise phrased in this way because I really wanted to be acknowledged for being just Avel. I got that praise more from my mom. My mom understood the distinction even if she never explicitly knew how it was important to me. Sometimes when I hear some one call me "Senator Gordly" I just want to run and say, "Stop! I'm Avel. Remember what's on the birth certificate? The one with the little feet: Avel Louise, 7 pounds 12 ounces. That's me! Grown-up version." Jasper's question over time has led me to a deeper spiritual journey of self understanding, including the teachings of the Dalai Lama, Deepak Chopra, and Don Miguel Ruiz. For the past fourteen years, I have embraced membership in the United Church of Christ at Highland Christian Center, pastored by Rev. Dr. W. G. Hardy, Jr., a ministry that embraces all people, especially young people.

Another part of the answer to Jasper's question came from a new job opportunity with the American Friends Service Committee (AFSC), a Quaker organization focused historically on peace, social justice, and war-related relief work. I got a call from Elizabeth Groff; "Buff" we called her, Buff Groff. She was director of the Southern Africa Program and she reached out to me in 1983 for support of that work. Another part of the answer came from my work with the Black United Front (BUF), especially the Saturday School Program, for which I served as coordinator. Over the course of the 1980s, my work with AFSC and the BUF became more tightly intertwined and mutually reinforcing.

Saturday School was especially thrilling because we demonstrated that there was a community of concern among parents about the quality of public education, particularly the curriculum touching African Americans. As coordinator, I pulled the right folks together who helped identify resources, like locations in the community where we could conduct classes. We located nearly a dozen churches, community centers, and other different locations in Northeast Portland. We recruited volunteers to serve at each location. Among the volunteers were parents and others from the community who were drawn to service. Because parents knew the work of the Black United Front, they trusted us enough to show up at these different sites with their children. We also needed a curriculum. Part of the team included experts, like Joyce Harris from the Black Educational Center, to write curriculum in math, reading, and African American history and culture. This program was available on Saturdays and included breakfast and lunch. The quality of support that we got from the community was huge; hundreds of people volunteered to make it all work. It was absolutely thrilling.

The Front was a core group of us who had stepped forward in the late 1970s to make fundamental change in the public school system. Our efforts included boycotts and demonstrations, school board meetings, and lots of hard work. I served on the Portland Public Schools Desegregation Monitoring Advisory Committee (DMAC) for five years, including a stint as vice-chair; Front member the late Halim Rahsaan (a well-known educational advocate) served as DMAC chair for many years. The Front's founder, Ronnie Herndon, recognized my administrative skills early on. He also understood that people in the community would respond to a call from me for volunteering. He was the one who asked me if I would serve as Saturday School coordinator.

Ronnie asked me in to Saturday School but what kept me coming back every week was the kids. They kept showing up. Their parents came with them. We had Black parents and we had white parents. White parents wanted to know why all students weren't getting exposure to this curriculum as a matter of course. Those parents became allies in our work to pressure the school district to address curricular deficiency. All of this work later informed my efforts in the legislature around curriculum, teacher preparation, cultural competence, and college opportunity. But what kept me energized at the time was always those kids.

One of my roles on Saturday was to go around and see how each site was doing and make sure that they had all their students, supplies, and everything else that we told parents we were going to deliver. We raised funds. People also gave us all kinds of things: pencils, paper, books. One man donated calculators for every child in the program. We were very much supported by community. There was a lot of press about Saturday School in Northeast Portland, especially our locations at St. Andrews Church, at Mallory Avenue Christian Church, at Redeemer Lutheran Church, and Matt Dishman Community Center, St. Phillip the Deacon Church, and Highland United Church of Christ.

We had both individuals and organizations as part of the Front. The Front included Rev. Jackson, Ronnie, Halim, Kamau Sadiki— who later led Portlanders Organized for Southern African Freedom (POSAF)— and Ben Priestley, who edited the *Front Page* newspaper, which became the national organ of the BUF, published in Portland. Richard Brown—who focused on police issues, police brutality, a community foot patrol, and community organizing (he was also a highly skilled photographer)—Charlotte Rutherford, Jean Vessup, Evelyn Crews (who later became my first legislative assistant), and Karen Powell, with whom I worked with at AFSC, stand out in my mind. Karen and her assistant Sherrian Haggar developed a system for tracking suspensions and expulsions in her role as AFSC's education program director. She later came to work with me to Salem as a legislative assistant as well and her work at AFSC informed my legislative agenda. The national Black United Front headquarters was in Chicago and we had our political conventions there and in East St. Louis, D.C., and Detroit. Locally we had members from the Albina Ministerial Alliance, sororities, fraternities, the Urban League of Portland, and the NAACP; that was the whole notion behind

"United" Front. Ronnie had earned the trust of the community from his founding of the Black Educational Center and as director of Albina Head Start. For many years, our local meetings took place at my house and at one point I was elected vice president for International Affairs of the National BUF organization.

Much of our power and success in organizing was through our regular Thursday night public meetings. People knew that they could count on a place in the community where they could come and get good information, information they could trust from people that they trusted. Those meetings were where it all happened. And there were many, many, many times when hundreds of people turned out for meetings, with the room just packed out! The Black United Front had tentacles into all the different organizations and places in the community. If the organization issued a call that people needed to show up at a school board meeting or in front of the police station or wherever needed, the call would go through all those organizations that participated in the Front and the call would go out to churches. We had whole families involved, like the beloved late Bobbie Jackson and her daughter Venita Myrick and son Charles Myrick, and on and on …

The BUF was community-based organizing. A couple of us had attended the Center for Third World Organizing training in Oakland, California; I was a product of that training. Ramón Ramirez of PCUN (Piñeros y Campesinos Unidos de Noroeste) and I were in the same class. That's where our friendship started. That friendship put us on the path to doing the work in the legislature around farmworkers and migrant rights. And when we started our Saturday School program, PCUN organizers would come up and serve as volunteers with us because they wanted to learn the model so they could take it back to the valley and replicate it. And they did.

My work with AFSC had introduced me to the phrase "third world," which I came to understand as a reference to indigenous people of color from throughout the underdeveloped world. Though I had heard Angela Davis and Stokely Carmichael speak and had read the work of Sonia Sanchez and Nikki Giovanni, I never developed any kind of analysis of my own about race and global structures of power. I would claim this as one of the holes in my educational and political development to this day. Nonetheless, at the AFSC, the Third World Caucus was a space to make visible the leadership and intellectual work of people of color within the organization. The caucus thus corrected a deficit in the organization long familiar to my lived experience in predominantly white Oregon. In the caucus and at AFSC, my voice was not only invited in but expected to be heard.

So, too, with the BUF. Our Saturday School was 100 percent volunteer-run. After a point, we couldn't sustain it. Yet we successfully made our point with the school board and district: there was a need not just for a curriculum on African American history and culture but in fact for a broader curriculum focused on the contributions of all people of color. Saturday School was picked up again later, in the 1990s, after I was elected to the legislature. I had gone to work with Albina Head Start as coordinator of their parent program. That job was a wonderful opportunity to help parents become more deeply involved with the Head Start organization and in the local public schools. In part, Saturday School augmented the work of the Education Crisis Team (also founded in the 1990s). Led by Ronnie Herndon and Tony Hopson of Self Enhancement, Inc., the Crisis Team pressed the public school system for a culturally relevant curriculum, teacher quality, more African American administrators, and attention to race in school expulsion rates. We never really went away.

Back in the early 1980s, I had responded to Buff Groff's phone call to connect with the American Friends Service Committee. She invited me to apply for a position, associate director of the Southern Africa program. The Quaker interview process felt like a lifetime. There were well over twenty interviews for a part-time job! I could not believe it. It was so different from anything I had ever experienced. Their process was for candidates to be interviewed by the executive committee, then the program committee, and in a number of other different settings. The process introduced me to the practice of consensus decision making. And at the end of that process I was one of the family. Not a Quaker, though, still a Baptist! I can't say that I actually enjoyed all of it but I learned so much about people—and myself—along the way. When it was all said and done the process was very much worth it.

Initially, Buff and I shared the position. As she decided to put in less time and then move on, I took on the role of director of the program. I was very excited to be in touch with the African continent; I knew I would be traveling back and forth to Philadelphia for quarterly meetings. Eventually I discovered that the job meant a great deal of travel, including to New York City and Washington, D.C., as well, and even to Africa. I usually took red-eye flights and it was exhausting. The travel proved a hardship, as it took me away from Ty, now a growing teenager, and home and family.

AFSC was in a process of redefining empowerment. It was an organization long accustomed to a paternalistic approach. There had to be a reckoning with that approach, because it was an affront to communities of color, who said: "We know our needs. We know what will work to address our needs. If you will invest in what we've identified as the solution, then we have a partnership. But if you are coming to say you know what's best and you want us to do it this way, then we're going to have a struggle." This approach had been a problem in the century behind us and we could not go forward into the new one in that way. Fortunately now the AFSC had people of color in leadership roles who were also in leadership roles within their community. Together, we brought this message to AFSC.

We who were in leadership roles but not necessarily in power roles at AFSC devised a Third World Caucus where we could talk together about issues and how they could be addressed within the organization. The caucus was in existence when I came on board. Yet we also felt that the Third World Caucus could be easily marginalized and segregated, keeping us busy without requiring that the organization take ownership of what we brought forward. This dynamic worked its way through the AFSC with people of color and with gays and lesbians, whose issues were also coming to the fore.

Redefining power and empowerment meant a very exciting time in the organization but also a very demanding and draining time.

AFSC affirmed for me the power of consensus—if you can get there—and the practice of listening. Power in the practice of listening. I learned that listening is something I practice well. The organization also deeply valued different perspectives and the importance of each person's life story. Life stories convey our worldview and the time and patience we invest in really listening to someone else's story shapes the quality of the relationship. Working with AFSC, I learned that I have patience, that I have persistence, and that I enjoy deep listening. These things have served me very well in the legislature and in my life.

REFERENCES
Kunjufu, Jawanza. *Developing Positive Self-Images and Discipline for Black Children.* Sauk Village, Illinois: African American Images, 1984.
———. *Countering the Conspiracy to Destroy Black Boys.* Sauk Village, Illinois: African American Images, 1985.
Sanchez, Sonia. *I've Been a Woman: New and Selected Poems.* Chicago, Illinois: Third World Press, 1978.

CHAPTER EIGHT

Forward Together, Backward Never

The visible leadership of the Black United Front was male. This meant Ronnie Herndon, the late Rev. John Jackson, the late Halim Rahsaan, Kamau Sadiki, and Richard Brown. Jean Vessup coordinated a lot of the BUF work around civil rights and police issues. She was an amazing organizer, hard worker, and good friend. Yet it was almost tradition that women worked in the background doing research, preparing for meetings, and making sure that things like press conferences happened. I was doing a lot of that work in the background, as were Karen Powell and Charlotte Rutherford, before she left for Howard University Law School. So were my good friends Evelyn Crews and Venita Myrick, and her mother Bobbie, and Elaine Harrison. Mrs. Bobbi Gary, Gloria Johnson, Mrs. Vivian Richardson, and Mrs. Vesia Loving also stand out in my memories.

All of us were called to service. We all signed on for the mission and vision of BUF, with its upbeat motto *Forward Together, Backward Never.* Over time, I became part of the more visible, before-the-cameras team at the press conferences, for example, or in a delegation to meet with the mayor. One day, I was talking with a Front supporter, Jean Drew, who worked at Portland Community College. I had recently wound up in more of an out-front role than usual and she commented: "Oh, now the fellas are letting you in." I remember that her comment struck a chord in me, like "Yeah, they are." It was not a criticism from her but it wasn't quite an affirmation either. At another BUF meeting at the King Neighborhood Facility, the topic being discussed was reproductive rights. After a time, I heard myself say, "You know, all the folks talking are men so far in this conversation and I'm really interested to know what the women around the table think about all of this." I felt the situation was odd and strange and needed to be interrupted and challenged. And the women did speak.

There was respect in BUF yet at the same time sexism in terms of the roles that folks just kind of fell into—or were asked to fill. Those of us who were conscious of it bumped up against it, and did not play along. At another meeting at my house, we were assembling packets for a public meeting. We were literally doing this assembly work on the floor with our chairs pushed back. The folks doing the work on the floor were the women and the guys were sitting back on chairs. We said, "Oh, no. This isn't going to work. You've got to work too. This is a work party. We're all in this together." So we put them to work. There was a lot of teasing and laughter. It was a little "gotcha" but at the same time an important recognition of the disrespectful assumption that only the women were going to be working on their hands and knees.

In BUF my leadership was affirmed. I was never co-chair of the organization, but I was asked to take on coordinating kinds of roles and I was seen as a leader. We held elections for co-chairs, and for secretary. Our longtime secretary was the late Mrs. Vivian Richardson. We always called her Mrs. Richardson, not Vivian, but Mrs. Richardson, as a sign of respect. The elections were more like affirmations of leadership rather than voting for rival slates. We were all also very conscious that Ronnie and Rev. Jackson had their lives on the line. They were getting death threats at their homes and death threats at their offices. There was fear. So there was a deep, deep, deep respect for these two men and the roles that they took on and a lot of love and concern for their families.

As I recalled with Richard Brown just the other day: "That time was a magical time." It will never be repeated in the same way. We had people who had a consciousness; who loved Black people and who loved themselves. They were clear about identity. We knew who we were and we were not ashamed. We were not afraid. Or if we had fear, there was a place to speak about that. We had honesty with and were accountable to one another. We all practiced these values faithfully for years and years. I haven't seen or experienced anything like that since, in terms of the integrity and quality of an organization and the respect that the organization earned in the eyes of the community, both the Black community and the broader community. We operated with strong principles.

Our maturity as individuals and collectively came from the fact that we met frequently, at least once a week. And there was a public meeting, where you had to be accountable, you just had to be. For a number of years, the smaller group meetings were at my house. Sometimes they were at Halim's home. By meeting in a private home, we could be open and frank and constructively critical. I learned to receive and give constructive criticism and came to deeply understand critique as a way to grow and find out who you are and what you are made of. What made the organization strong and dependable was the accountability of a core group of people to one another and to the community. In this way we got good things done. We sponsored a community unity day at Jefferson High School for several years and held fundraisers at social clubs on Alberta. We worked for justice and corrected things that were wrong, whether it meant police issues, educational issues, economic opportunity, or housing. The foundation for that work was built on a strong group of people.

I attended the second official meeting of the BUF, in 1979; a group had met in 1978, but this second meeting really started to live out the vision. The hard-core membership was made up of people who were fearless and kept coming back to do the work. Historically it was a small group of people, perhaps twenty-five or so, that ebbed and flowed. Beyond that were the supporters, who would come to the Thursday night meetings. That was always the time to take the temperature of the community and that's also where accountability came in. We didn't do anything without checking in and finding out how the community wanted to move. There was also a group of folks who were white who wanted to participate in the organization. We established a group of allies, but they didn't come to our regular, smaller membership meetings. I appreciated that support but we wanted to keep the allies separate so that we could have frank discussions and so our agenda would not be diffused or changed.

My connection to the BUF shifted a bit when I started working with the Urban League. The Black United Front was a confrontational group. It did not rely only on confrontational style or tactics to get things done but if confrontation was needed, BUF would go for it. The Urban League had a different approach. I remember a protest at a school board meeting while I was working for the Urban League. I was present and had arranged for other people to be present. But the folks who actually carried out the demonstration with the signs and the more in-your-face kind of stuff, those were Front members right down in the front of the room. The roles were understood. The Urban League was doing it the way they did it, present and supportive; and the Front folks did their thing. There may have been those who just looked at it all and said, "That's the Black United Front, period." In a sense that's what it was, since the Black United Front brought together all community-based organizations who wanted to have a voice. The Albina Ministerial Alliance and NAACP were in the room as well. In some ways, it was all the Black United Front.

Our leadership was highly coordinated and mutually supportive. During anti-apartheid demonstrations the Portland police chief asked our leaders to call them off. They invited us to meet and we did. We met at an establishment that served alcohol and I remember that they wanted us to have something to drink. None of us went for that. Then there was an offer of trips to South Africa so we could actually see what it was really like there. We said no to that, too. Our leadership certainly had disagreements. Demonstrations were absolutely planned but at one protest there was someone prominent who wanted to be arrested on the spot. I wanted to let it happen. Ronnie disagreed. "No, we shouldn't. We've got a plan; gotta stick to it." I remember the rub at the time. We talked about it afterwards: when we have a plan we have to stick to it. He emphasized that we could never know what someone else's motives might be for wanting to be involved and how important it was to maintain control. I maybe brooded for a while and then questioned what that person did have in their mind about being arrested. It also put me in touch with my desire to go off script and go for the moment.

Outside of formal meetings and demonstrations I became aware that people trusted me. I regularly was called on, consulted, and confided in. Then I started to think that sometimes maybe a person can just know too much. Trust became an issue for me. Who could I trust, beyond the immediate circle of people I really knew? We had gone and would go to the mat together. But what if the city had a file on me? Is the phone tapped? Is someone with binoculars watching me? A kind of paranoia set in. I really started to worry about my privacy. At the same time, I knew trusted members of my community were watching out for me. Like the late Bill McClendon. He knew my father well (McClendon had worked on the railroad). He was also a musician; he played piano. Back in the day he had owned a club; he had a newspaper and later taught at Reed College. So as I moved into my different roles in the community, Bill McClendon always kept kind of an eye on me. When I was at the Urban League, he would drop by from time to time and he would sit and unload wisdom and I would just listen. That connection was part of the magical time. I had someone of McClendon's brilliance keeping a hand on me that said: You are one of the community's chosen. We want to give you all we have; we want to pour everything we have into you.

Bill McClendon would come by my Urban League office to talk about what was going on in the community, and to talk about the old days. He'd tell me about my mom and dad's past, and the politics of the day. And always, always, something about our history and culture as a people. Sometimes he'd just have a question. "What did I think about this or that?" Once he asked me about the United Negro College Fund and their slogan: *A mind is a terrible thing to waste.* He said that he so disliked that motto. He thought that it should say, "It's a terrible thing to waste a mind," which is better grammar and more vivid phrasing. That was his point. We can do better and we always have to be pushing ourselves to do better. That's why he came to my office, to remind me. I don't know that I was fully conscious of the gift Bill McClendon gave me during those conversations. I most certainly am now.

After I left the Urban League, my position at the AFSC gave me a wonderful opportunity to travel to Southern Africa. I was hired as director of the Southern Africa Program. It was 1984 or '85, just before my mom passed. I went for three weeks and visited South Africa, Mozambique, Zimbabwe, Lesotho, and Botswana. We were there at a time of war. The war was being fought in South Africa against its own people as well as in the neighboring so-called front line states. There was loss of life and destruction, including bombings of houses and other establishments. We had been invited to attend a conference that was being led by Bishop Desmond Tutu. The "we" included Jerry Herman, national director of the Southern Africa Program for AFSC, Shaka Kusaidi, also from Philadelphia and a local organizer for AFSC; and Randy Carter, director of the Southern Africa Program out of the Seattle AFSC office. Two other folks from the Philadelphia office were also with us for a very short time at the beginning of our trip. During this trip we had meetings with folks from every walk of life—government, civic, church, and business— and including everyday people. Jerry drove most of the time. When it was time to go to the conference in South Africa, we went by car, leaving from Harare, Zimbabwe. Along the way, we were stopped several times at gunpoint. Due to the volatility of the region we were suspect, four Black people in a car traveling along the road.

Early on in the trip we realized that we were being watched. At one point, we decided to get rid of all our anti-apartheid literature. We just tore it all up and threw it out the window, so fearful were we that it could bring harm to us if we were stopped. The first checkpoint from Zimbabwe into South Africa wasn't really a checkpoint. The first stop was by Black South African military police who just came up behind us quickly and ordered us to stop the car. We did. There was not a lot of traffic. We had to get out of the car. They searched the car and they searched our luggage, item by item. I can even remember them going through my tampon box and the individual pages of my books. Then we got back in the car and drove away. After this first stop we got rid of all the literature.

There was another stop. We were headed down to the Transkei, the place where Nelson Mandela was born. Shaka wanted to get some postage and so we wound up stopping on a street in the Transkei. A vehicle came up behind us. We were ordered to follow the vehicle. Another armed car carrying two people followed us. We traveled out of town and went for a long, long drive until we got to this little place out in the wilderness. There was nothing else around, just this little house. We went into the house. Each of us was separately interrogated in English. They asked us: "Where are you from? Where are going?" We were interrogated by a person they called Major Fatman. I kid you not. That name sticks in my memory because it was so outrageous—and probably phony, intended to throw us off. Nobody else knew where we were at this point. I was terrified.

Time went by and they finally established that we could leave. But Major Fatman wanted us to go back into Transkei. His wife had a shop there and he wanted us to go by and say hello to his wife. We agreed to do this. How ironic, since we had just been there! We drove down the highway again. Then I realized that I didn't have my passport. We had to go back! We eventually arrived in the Transkei and we went to the shop. A very charming woman helped us there.

Of course, we decided to find something to buy! Then night fell on our second night in the Transkei. We had not been able to get a room the previous night; the hotel keeper was afraid to rent to us. We went back on the road again and decided that we could not go to the conference. We felt we were being monitored. We cancelled our visits with other people on our list in South Africa because we didn't want to bring harm to them.

Back out on the road, we got surrounded by South African military police. This time, they were all white except for one Black man. We all got pulled out of the car, searched again; all of our clothing down to the pages of books. We were separated on a road with no lighting and no traffic. I was trembling, literally quaking.

Later Jerry and Shaka also said that they quaked with fear. The police had uzis trained on us. The Black man had a shotgun and at one point he asked each of us if we knew Muhammad Ali. That was the impossibly funny moment in this crisis. What would be the right answer, I wondered? Another ironic element was that it was the Fourth of July. But dark. They kept us out for what seemed like forever—maybe an hour or so we figured later. When they established that we were Americans—and African Americans—they let us go.

Jerry drove like a bat out of hell. We drove and drove and drove. We got to a place called Port St. John on the Indian Ocean. We needed a place to stay. Luckily we found a little hotel with a liquor store right next door that was open. While we were driving, we were hysterical, absolutely hysterical. Literally laughing and crying. At the liquor store we each got our own bottle. We went next door to get our rooms. There was a little patio area where we all sat down together. We had an amazing view of the ocean. As we drank, we went over the events: "Did that really happen?" "What did they say?" We played it all back: what we heard, what we saw, what we felt. Over and over and over. We were very grateful to have a place to lay our heads because we had been awake for so long. Then, during the night, there was an explosion. We found out later that it was the boiler or something innocent in the hotel, but in the moment, I feared the worst.

The next day we considered going to the American embassy to tell them about the things that had happened to us. We questioned their possible response. The stops were never about paying a toll or being shaken down for money. We were targeted politically. But then again we were there opposed to U.S. foreign policy toward South Africa. We were on a fact-finding mission for an organization, the American Friends Service Committee, whose opposition was on the record. We did not think we were going to find a friend at the embassy. We decided to just keep going, keep driving, and get back to Zimbabwe. There we could get on our flight and get going home. We flew from Zimbabwe to Johannesburg. In the airport, we were in quarantine for hours. They had people cordoned off. Everyone was being watched carefully and our luggage was searched again. In the Johannesburg airport I met Bayard Rustin. Rustin was a long-time civil rights and human rights activist who had played a significant role in the 1963 March on Washington for Jobs and Freedom. I found out much later that he was in South Africa "under the auspices of the International Rescue Committee, which had refugee camps in Lesotho and Swaziland." No doubt we had visited some of the same camps in Lesotho. Rustin was seated at a table near us at the airport, having a meal. The day we flew out was the same day that the state of emergency was declared in South Africa. When I looked down from the airplane and saw fires in different places, I felt a strange rush of adrenalin. Every muscle in my body was tired or hurting.

Before our abrupt exit from South Africa, however, our group managed to learn a great deal. We visited refugee camps and health clinics. We saw soldiers hurt and maimed who faced a lack of medical care. In Botswana, we visited a bombed-out place where nuns had lived. In the debris were glass and paper and pieces of books … and bloodstains; the bombing was so recent. We talked to young people who had escaped the war zones with their lives. Violence and fear of violence in South Africa pushed people into refugee camps. A very striking feature of those young people—teenagers, really—was their knowledge about the anti-apartheid movement in the United States. They actually knew about the different marches and demonstrations and other things that were going on. They thanked us and acknowledged us. There was such deep irony in what we were hearing from them and in what they gave us, when I thought about the young people at home. I thought especially about young men who were engaged in gang wars, who did not have a clue about identity and who instead played out their confusion around turf and drugs. The young men of similar age in the refugee camps of southern Africa were fighting for something that we took for granted: freedom. It was too much. It was overwhelming.

That's the story I came back with and shared. We were living our lives in the U.S. while people were being murdered in southern

Africa fighting for their basic human rights. Our job was to bear witness to the lives that were being lost. There was a report from the conference and I don't remember that anyone else had the experience of surveillance and harassment that we did. Some in the AFSC southern Africa movement family had suggested that we not go. Going was dangerous and it seemed like the state of emergency was imminent. There was a debate in the movement at that time about going into South Africa at all. Some chose to go and witness, and come back with the stories. That's the side that we came down on. The movement was global and we each played our roles. We understood that we were acting as civil rights and human rights activists and that as Martin Luther King, Jr., taught us, "injustice anywhere is a threat to justice everywhere."

When I returned to Portland, I shared my story with *The Oregonian.* I appreciated the chance to put the message out there. As after my first visit to Africa in the 1970s, my return found me in a kind of depression. I had to decompress. I needed to process the reality of overabundance compared to places I'd seen where people just scraped out a daily living. It was just so much work to put all of that into some perspective. And my mother was ill. She had kidney disease and had been on dialysis for a number of years. Ty was in the Navy at this point; he was on a ship—and it was not a cruise. He almost traveled to Mombasa when I was abroad but the first Gulf War was upon him. Ty wrote me a letter telling me that Jesse Jackson had been right about war and that he wanted to come home and work for peace. He was anxious to get out of the Mediterranean.

The need to tell the story and decompress unfolded over the next few months. I had gatherings at my house. I had lots of slides from the trip, so I just invited a lot of people over. There were a lot of Front people in that group. I also presented at AFSC meetings. And I shared the story at the Oregon State Prison with inmates, sponsored by Uhuru Sasa, an inmate club. The next winter, I participated in a U.S. tour with a number of South Africans and South Africa freedom activists mainly focused on achieving divestiture. Our group was assigned to Iowa in the month of January, and we visited colleges, universities, civic organizations, and churches over a ten-day period. One of the South Africans I toured with was the exiled activist Dumasani Kumalo, a wonderful man who later came to Oregon to assist us with the divestiture effort in Salem.

One of the most lingering, haunting images from that Southern Africa trip was of a storage area where they kept different supplies for people in a refugee camp. I saw high mounds of a white substance. I couldn't figure out what the mounds were. I looked closer and realized that it was partially used bars of soap, from hotels. They had been shipped and packaged for re-use. My first thought while I actually, physically looked at the piles was: "Why can't these be new bars of soap?" And then, "What is it about a society that has so much to dispose of?" That image did something to my mind. It reminded me of those "white elephant" projects I had seen on my very first trip to Africa years before. What are these alien piles of whiteness doing on the African continent? Every time I travel and I'm in a hotel with that little bar of soap, I am immediately taken back to that mound in the refugee camp. It's impossible to break that connection in my mind. That image, like so many others from South Africa, changed me forever.

REFERENCES
Levine, Daniel. *Bayard Rustin and the Civil Rights Movement.* New Brunswick, New Jersey: Rutgers University Press, 2000.

CHAPTER NINE

A Heart for Africa

Everything about Africa has faces in it for me, and memories, from
time spent with young people in refugee camps and clinics in camps
short of supplies. Soldiers traumatized for life, given what they had
witnessed in battles in the front-line states, sat with us in outdoor
cafes and told us their stories. South African freedom was not
something happening "over there" to "those people." It was (and is)
very much in my heart. It's personal. I have South African friends like
ANC leader Thandi Luthuli-Gcabashe (daughter of the Nobel laureate
Chief Albert Luthuli) and Dumasani Kumalo, who had been in exile
for many, many years. I know their stories of not being able to go
home for the funerals of their mothers, fathers, and other family
members. During my anti-apartheid activism I shared their hope
and prayer that freedom would come while they were still alive.
The stories of Winnie Mandela and Miriam Makeba that I read also
inspired me greatly at this time.

As my work expanded its global reach, I still remained grounded
in local activism in Portland and, of course, in family. I lived in the
Northeast neighborhood, and after Ty completed his service on the
USS Ranger and joined the reserves, he lived with me for a time.
He worked at Delta Airlines as an aviation structural mechanic.
For a short while, he lived with his dad, who had separated from
his second wife for a time. I was active in the Black United Front
and most of my women friends were, too, like Jean Vessup, Karen
Powell, and Evelyn Crews. I had lost touch with my high school
and childhood friends but, with Gloria Gostnell, created a reading
group focused on Black women writers like bell hooks, Alice
Walker, Toni Morrison, and Paule Marshall, which was a key source
of nourishment. Faye also moved back to Portland from Eugene.
She and her husband Michael had a daughter Michelle. Michelle
became Ty's assistant in his magic act, which he performed at

105

birthday parties and at Saturday School. In this way, my family gave encouragement to my work, even as it sometimes took me far from home.

Joining the American Friends Service Committee meant working with an organization that was connected to Southern Africa, including the nation of South Africa. It was an amazing, wonderful, and historic opportunity. AFSC also provided support and resources to build a community-based organization that became Portlanders Organized for Southern African Freedom (POSAF). This work involved relationships established in and connected to the Black United Front and the Black Educational Center, and to other people who had an interest in Southern Africa. These groups now had a new place to focus their energy and concern. POSAF was that place. At the same time, people in Portland understood that the American Friends Service Committee made the community piece possible, through field support that sustained the organizing effort. It was hand in hand. That work lasted well over seven years, 1983-1990, and that's just counting my time on staff. The Southern Africa Program existed before my coming but the outreach into the local African American community still needed to be developed.

But the way had been prepared by leading clergy, especially Rev. Jackson. Rev. Jackson's voice and service were appreciated deeply throughout the church and wider community of Oregon. He was a warrior for social justice whose wisdom was often sought. His archive on the Portland Community College Campus (Cascade) reveals the breadth of his work, especially in education. Under his leadership, the Albina Ministerial Alliance was a unifying force for social justice. Rev. Jackson and his close colleague, Rev. Garlington, were recognized for their effectiveness in 1980 by the National Conference of Christians and Jews. By advocating for Head Start and seeking to secure justice for all citizens, they demonstrated an unswerving allegiance to high ideals: the release of human potential and the liberation of the human spirit.

Though I lacked a regular home church in these years, I paid attention to politics. One of the things I oversaw at AFSC was a legislative agenda, including a push to get Oregon businesses to divest from South Africa. We arranged for community folks to go to Salem to testify in support of divestiture legislation. Representative Jim Hill (of Salem) and Representative Margaret Carter (of Portland) had been working on a bill together. We supported their efforts as well as efforts in the community in favor of divestiture. We were able to apply a lot of pressure to make something happen in Salem. Through AFSC, we brought in speakers from South Africa like Neo Mnumzana, ambassador to the United Nations, and he provided testimony. Dumisani Kumalo, exiled from South Africa in 1979 and director of the U.S.-based American Committee on Africa and the Africa Fund, also came to Oregon, as did Thabo Mbeki, later elected president of South Africa. These men were very well regarded in the international movement against apartheid and they saw Oregon as a prime opportunity to make something happen. And we did.

We also made a careful and coordinated effort to force the resignation of the honorary consul for South Africa, Mr. Calvin Van Pelt, from his Portland office. From the very beginning, we called for his resignation. We committed to demonstrate every week, two or three times a week. We signed people up to be out there on the sidewalk. We had people signed up to be arrested. The message we put out through the media was that not only were we not going away but in fact, every time we came back, we'd be stronger. We always made sure that the folks who were being arrested were respectable citizens of Portland. BUF and AFSC sat down with police to make sure things went smoothly. We always wanted the police to know our people by name. We had identified security folks, wearing armbands, who had clear responsibilities. This way, the police knew that anything unlawful occurring was not by our people.

I was the lead organizer along with Kamau Sadiki, an engineer by profession and an instructor and board member at the Black Educational Center. Our people either had armbands or another clear designation, and we planned things sometimes right down to the clothes we wore. If we had a megaphone, that person was also designated (it was usually Charles Myrick). If somebody else came

with the megaphone, they were politely excused. Regular chants included: "We're fired up, can't take no more, won't stand no more!" "Africa for Africans," and "Free Nelson Mandela." "We're fired up!" especially stands out in my memory. We just wore Van Pelt down. He and the chief of police realized that this was a movement of people who weren't going away. And we could not be dismissed as a ragtag group of barefooted hippies who didn't have jobs and who were going to smoke a bunch of pot. We had people in suits with briefcases. And we made it very clear each time we marched that "we'll see you next time."

When we prevailed, there was exhilaration and relief, too. Whenever we protested publicly we felt responsible for the lives of the people who participated. I had to be discerning and always watchful. We had other eyes doing the same thing, but I was always very mindful. Our victory in Oregon was noted by Randall Robinson's organization, Transafrica. I remember getting a letter from Robinson congratulating us. It was huge news around the nation and I kept Robinson's letter tacked up to the wall in my home for a long time as a reminder that our work was tied to an international movement and that we had made a difference.

Portlanders Organized for Southern African Freedom met almost
weekly at the AFSC office on East Burnside Street. A number of
PSU students, some from African nations, were very involved in the
organization and participated in the demonstrations and rallies.
Kamau and Charles were trusted friends and also members of the
BUF. Kamau took his African name in the late 1970s; his given
name was Nathan Anderson. His wife, Mary Avery, took the name
Amina after they married. She later took a significant leadership
role heading up the Black United Fund of Oregon, which had also
been founded by Ronnie Herndon (around 1983). That philanthropic
organization is now over twenty-five years old. Kamau Sadiki and
Amina relocated to Washington, D.C., a few years ago, a huge loss
to the Black activist and cultural nationalist community of Portland.
The legacy of their work together to establish the Black United Fund
remains.

Parents who had children enrolled in the Black Educational
Center were also supportive and active with POSAF. Some white
allies included students from the various college campuses. Some
students and white allies were much too casual in their dress at
protests, literally unkempt and shoeless. We needed them to dress
in a manner to be taken seriously by passersby and by the media.
We recommended that participants dress as if they were going to
a job interview or to church. We had to be very clear about our
agenda and principles and who was in charge. We always dealt with
white individuals who came carrying signs about other agendas, like
socialism or communism, very respectfully. And no one ever got hurt.
Church members from Mt. Olivet Baptist and other congregations
also participated. Many Front members were also churchgoers.
Charles and Kamau for years led an African Liberation Day march
sponsored by the Black Educational Center. I always knew that
Kamau and Charles had my back in the different activist settings we
shared.

During Neo Mnumzana's visit, I was responsible for getting him
settled and for driving him back and forth from Salem. When he

learned that my mom was in the hospital, he wanted to go and see her before he did anything else. I took him to Emanuel Hospital. He sat at my mom's bedside and talked with her with reverence and with such grace, as though she were a queen. It was so wonderful; my mom was deeply moved by his compassion. To say that he was thoughtful would be an understatement; it was a deeply meaningful and graceful act on his part. Then he went to Salem, the state capitol, to meet our legislators. I remember sitting in the different offices and being struck by Neo's presence and his way of speaking. He was very intentional, very powerful; I felt like I was in the presence of greatness. Later his wife Susan came out to Oregon and she did her own speaking tour that included Mt. Olivet Baptist church.

As my African activism touched the state legislature, I learned several political lessons. In Salem I discovered the meaning of the old saying: "No permanent friends, no permanent enemies, only permanent interests." Representative Margaret Carter was the first African American woman legislator in Oregon, elected in a so-called Black district as a product of community organizing. She won her seat by defeating a number of Black and white men who also wanted it. Jim Hill had been elected in a very different district, Salem, which is predominantly white. I did not live in Carter's district but she hired my sister Faye Burch to serve as her legislative assistant for a time. Faye went on to advise a number of city and state elected officials on policy matters in addition to running her own business in the years to follow.

While some people in Oregon opposed divestiture, we did not spend a lot of energy focused on confronting that opposition. Sometimes the participants in the marches, rallies, or protests were kind of written off as being communist or Marxist. I didn't really put a lot of energy into focusing on these labels because such criticism never carried the day. One of our South Africa demonstrations brought out hundreds of people—we in POSAF always counted. But the TV news story, I think it was KC Cowan's report, said it was around fifty people. I called her up and asked, "How did you come up with fifty? That's not correct." By this kind of careful work I think

POSAF did a good job of being a credible organization. We had the participation of credible citizens of Portland, from different walks of life, and that carried the day.

I did encounter opposition in the capitol. We really wanted to push Governor Neil Goldschmidt on divestment. We had a conversation in Rep. Carter's office in which she asked us not to do that. We couldn't make that promise. I remember being surprised at her push back. She cautioned us about embarrassing the governor. POSAF didn't see it that way. We wanted him to be more aggressive regarding divestment. While a vote for divesture was not a career-breaker for any Oregon legislator at the time, I was still surprised that Carter, our Black community's representative, seemed to be more concerned about protecting the governor than taking even a symbolic stand for Black freedom. Even more prominent in my mind at the time was Goldschmidt's very troubling public statement about the leadership of the Black United Front. He commented that the BUF leadership—meaning Ronnie Herndon—needed to be "squashed." Goldschmidt used those exact words at a time when Ronnie was getting death threats. He and his family were afraid and a governor's words carried power.

Moreover some saw Goldschmidt as responsible for patronage and he took it upon himself to signal which Black folks were OK or not. His reputation among some Black folks was divided. Some saw him as an ally. There were others who saw through his charisma and said no, there's something else going on here and it's called paternalism. We're not going to play that game and we don't need a guiding hand for our agenda. Carter was loyal to Goldschmidt; I don't know that I'd ever even met him up to that point in time. But the incident was my first real encounter with raw politics, the politics of covering for and protecting people. On the one hand, there are issues, but on the other hand, other things get played out around issues. An issue around trust came up for me, and also loyalty. What was most important to Carter in that meeting was protecting the governor. Her position told me something about how I would be relating to her around this issue. This passage was more than just a bump in the road; it colored the way we related from that point forward. Then there was the famous phone call that wasn't really a phone call. A message had been left on my phone at AFSC. Carter probably thought that the phone had been hung up but she was still talking to Jim Hill in the background and the machine continued to record their back and forth. I heard them say: "What the hell are they [POSAF] doing?" and why were we doing it the way we were doing it? One of my take-aways from overhearing that conversation was the need to take care of misinformation. It was a teachable moment.

I developed a public identity around South African freedom. There were folks who started to call me "Miss POSAF." Mrs. Vivian Richardson would always say: "Here comes Miss POSAF. What are we supposed to do today?" People understood that I was director of the Southern Africa program for AFSC, had played other roles for AFSC, and that I was also identified publicly with POSAF—Portlanders Organized for Southern African Freedom. To Mrs. Richardson, that made me "Miss POSAF." She and other people responded when the call came to act. I felt honored by the responsibility but was also conscious that people asked me to take on different—and difficult— roles. At times, I also felt burdened, burned out, and isolated. I also was grappling with depression. When I was fully awake, so to speak, there was joy; the joy that comes from helping to make important things happen and being a part of helping to make things happen. But there was also the burden of responsibility; the weight of knowing that people are looking to you, or leaning on you, and their expectation is that you're going to make things happen.

For me, "making things happen" meant identifying talent. I learned how to bring people together to unleash that talent together; and I know deeply all the wonderful things that flow from such synergies. I was taught how to make things happen. One of the things that Ronnie was really good about was providing mentoring and training for the Black United Front. We did time management training more than once. I received the same kind of time-management training that an executive would receive. I relied on my day timer. The training Ronnie practiced with Albina Head

Start he carried over into the Front. We all had day timers and kept our calendars. We had lists. We had a phone tree—I mean a really good phone tree. We had ways of holding ourselves accountable and one another accountable. The fact that we met regularly every week on a Thursday kept us accountable and helped us internalize certain behaviors.

I really enjoyed the strategy sessions—not so much because I considered myself, then or now, to be a good strategic thinker—but I'm a good listener. I grew to appreciate how important it is to have people in a group who are doing the listening. It's important to reflect back, to ask questions, and to examine assumptions. I enjoyed doing that. I enjoy just mixing it up and saying, at the point where everybody's saying, "Yeah, we got it all figured out" "Oh really? Well, what if ..." Or "Have we thought about ...?" I really enjoyed doing that. I often had the responsibility of notifying the media about out activities through press releases, media releases, and press conferences. I wrote some of the statements and coordinated all of that work. The resulting relationships served BUF well. There was a period of a few years where we knew reporters who covered local issues fairly, like Lars Larson. Especially telling is a little-known and well-produced video called "Reading, Writing, and Racism," generated by channel 12 KPTV with Larson. I enjoyed building relationships that allowed us to advance the work of our organizations; it earned a lot of respect for the work. We were known as people who were serious and who were to be reckoned with seriously.

Part of our seriousness also derived from a key Black civil rights tradition: the mass meeting. Mass meetings were a way to educate and hear back from the community about how folks wanted to move forward. The meetings also became opportunities for media connection because the press had access to come in to photograph or write a story. I can't remember a time when we said that the press couldn't come in to a mass meeting. The mass meeting was an element of the civil rights movement that we definitely carried forward. We worked very intentionally with the press as our partner to help us market this program because we needed the help of the community. We needed volunteers, materials, and supplies for Saturday School. We needed people to know about our progress and accomplishments around South African freedom. There was actually a fabulous relationship with the media about our work.

At the moment that Nelson Mandela was freed on February 11, 1990, I was on the phone. It was early in the morning. It was a three-way call between Joyce Harris, Kamau Sadiki, and myself. We were crying. We were watching TV at the same time when Nelson Mandela and Winnie walked out of jail together. It was just totally unbelievable. We cried and cried and cried. We also planned a community celebration at the Matt Dishman Community Center while on the phone together. We had a huge turnout of community people. We replayed the tape of Nelson Mandela coming out of prison. We had music, we had food, we had stories, we had a high celebration. It was just amazing. There was joy, joy, joy! People were almost giddy. We danced the "Toyi Toyi," a South African dance used in protests during the apartheid era. There was another celebration at King School. And as I recall, Barbara Roberts spoke; she was then Secretary of State (and soon to be governor). But what impressed me most that day was being at King elementary school and having the children present to participate in making history. Later, when South Africans had that first vote for Mandela and people saw those lines and heard about the hours that people had stood in line—that's another memory that's just seared in my mind.

My mother did not live to see this triumph. When Mom passed, I was not at home. I was in Chicago, at a conference related to peace and justice work. I have convinced myself—and my sister tells me—that it was OK with Mom, too, that I went to the conference. Mom did not want me to worry about her but I actually had years of guilt for not being at home when she passed. When I left for Chicago, Mom was in the hospital. And she was low. During the conference I went to a park by the waterfront, and I remember that a feeling just came to me. I looked at the sky and in that moment I knew that I needed to call home. I called my mom's house first and didn't get an answer. Then I called the hospital. I asked about my mom. The person on the other end of the line hesitated, so I knew. Then I got my sister and she told me she had passed. I was with a friend, Dr. Conrad Worrill, Chair of the National Black United Front, and the person who actually made my arrangements to go home. He stayed with me until it was time to get on the plane. Mom was gone when I came home.

I went over and over her death and my absence in my head for a long time. Then I just didn't let myself think about how I should have been home, at her bedside. I prayed for forgiveness. My sister really helped me with that one. There was a beautiful service for her. Mom was a member of the Eastern Star, so all of the women in white showed up and took over in their grand way, graceful way, beautiful way. Mom had been Grand Worthy Matron and they treated her like the queen that she was. I have no memory of the rituals they performed during the funeral, just of these beautiful women in white surrounding her casket. Ty came home on leave from the Navy and he was also wearing his whites. I do have a sharp memory, during the funeral, of someone wailing. The wail just went through my heart. And then I realized it was my sister. She and Mom had such a special relationship. They were just so close, so close. Fayetta was sitting with my mother-in-law, Ty's grandmother, Ethel, and in my mind I see Ethel putting her arm around my sister and comforting her. My mother was loved by so many people in the community. She had worked in Neighborhood Bill's grocery store for years, so kids knew her and parents knew her. Everybody knew Mom. She was this beautiful, graceful, peaceful presence with a sense of humor. To this day, that's what we hear about her from folks who knew her and loved her.

Years later, I recognized that, for a while after Mom's death, I had just checked out. I remember that a stack of mail piled up. I found some way to function, but there was just so much pain that I didn't deal with. When I finally opened that mail, I found notes and expressions about my mother that were just beautiful; really, really beautiful. At the time, however, I didn't really grieve. It came later. In fact, I was in New York State at the Peg Leg Bates Retreat Center for the National Black Holistic Conference. Betty Shabazz, Malcolm X's widow, was there as was sisterfriend Iyanla Vanzant, the charismatic spiritual teacher, Susan Taylor, *Essence Magazine* editor, and Third World Press founder Haki Madhubuti. That's where it all came out. I went with some folks from home: Amina and Kamau Sadiki, the late gifted artist Charlotte Lewis, Adriene Cruz, Guyann Herndon, and the late Omotoyo Fletcher. Omotoyo (her name was Julia but she was known as Omotoyo) knew my mom and my grandmother. At one point at this retreat, we were all seated in a circle and we started to sing "Wade in the water." Part of the ritual involved actually walking to the water. And as I started to sing this song, the grief came up and over me and I just fell into Omotoyo's arms. I'd always seen her as Mom, and related to her as a mother. I fell into her arms. And she knew. She knew what it was and she just rocked me, just rocked me.

REFERENCES
"Honorary Consul to South Africa Resigns," *The Oregonian*, 19 January 1985.
"Bill to Force State Sale of South Africa-Related Stocks Faces Fight," *The Oregonian*, 13 February 1987.
Vanzant, Iyanla. *Acts of Faith: Daily Meditations for People of Color*. Fireside, 1993.

CHAPTER TEN

Hope and Hard Work

Back when Nelson Mandela was released in 1990, I was aware
that people in my community viewed me as a leader, as a source
of good counsel, and as someone to be trusted. I was someone
they consulted with on a number of issues, aside from U.S. policy
towards South Africa. For example, Bishop Wells, leader of the Albina
Ministerial Alliance (and lead/founding pastor at Emanuel Temple
Church of God in Christ), would call on me about issues in the
community. I can vividly remember a woman who worked with the
state employment agency with whom we sat for a long time to come
up with a strategy to help her stay in her job. Ronnie, Rev. Jackson,
and Rev. Garlington (but especially Ronnie) regularly called on me
to participate in significant decisions, discussion sessions, and press
conferences. In these meetings I was always aware, looking around
the table, of being if not the only woman, maybe one of two or three
women. Depending on the issue, some other women consulted
included Karen Powell, Jean Vessup, Charlotte Rutherford, Edna
Robertson, Mrs. Vesia Loving, or Mrs. Bobbi Gary.

My awareness of this imbalance produced an ongoing
consciousness in my work. I was very conscious of not allowing
myself to be put in the position of being the note taker or the one
who would wind up with more than my share of the work. Halim
Rahsaan liked to write and was often the one who said: "Maybe we
need to write a letter ..." about this or that. In my mind, I'd think:
"That's good. Let the guys have a share of the work." It is important
for me to make the point that I did and still do support advancing
effective African American male leadership. It is so important to have
these positive, powerful images successfully confronting injustice
before our children. We always, always need a counter to the
pervasive images that emasculate Black men in Portland, Oregon, and
elsewhere. So therein lies the tension, sometimes, between affirming

male leadership and Black women asserting their leadership and having it affirmed.

Sharing power and labor was negotiated informally in community settings, both within and outside the Black United Front. There were times, for example, when Ronnie couldn't chair meetings or facilitate, so he would ask me to do that. There were other men who could have taken on the role but he asked me, so I took the requests as a statement about trust. It was also a statement about my capacity to be effective and I got a reputation of getting things done. People let me know that they appreciated how I moved things along without a heavy hand and how I made sure everybody had a voice. People left meetings feeling good, like something had been accomplished. As my skills developed, I was being affirmed and acknowledged.

Accepting my own skills and power had its challenges. At one press conference in particular, a picture really told the story. I was asked to participate in this media event but I was trying not to be on stage and it shows. The photograph is of Garlington, Jackson, and Herndon but I'm pulling myself back, out of the picture. There were four seats at the table but I was literally pulling myself back; like I just wanted to be in the background. When I think back on that picture, I remember wondering: "Why am I pulling myself back?" At the time, I didn't have an answer. A few years later, another picture appeared in *The Oregonian*, in the Metro Section. We were confronting then-mayor Bud Clark about affirmative action. In this scenario—Ronnie was there—I'm very much present and very much on board. I even remember that I had a suit on! I was dressed for battle, though my preferred dress is casual. (I've had folks give me suits to wear at different times, a not so subtle commentary on my preferred attire!) With Mayor Clark, Ronnie and I were on purpose, we were being taken seriously, and I'm not holding back. In the other picture I'm holding back.

In those same years I have a strong memory of my mom and her pride. I remember her being very proud of the work of the Black United Front. She was a reader, so she read the community newspapers papers like *The Skanner* and *The Observer*, as well as accounts of our activities in *The Oregonian* and on TV, too. She had such pride in this group of younger folks, of which her daughter was one, who were out there stirring the pot and doing it for all the right reasons. I remember her pride, and that of her generation of churchgoers. Whenever we were out in the community, at the grocery store or even on the street, folks had a way of saying, "Y'all keep that up!" or "Be careful out there." I'd hear that, too. Folks had a way of letting us know that they approved; disapproval among Black people was rare. Some were made afraid by the confrontational style of the Front; they feared for retaliation against us or that disturbing the status quo would elicit other attacks.

Throughout my active years with the Front—with Mandela's release almost right in the middle, in 1990—the focus was on education. It culminated with the creation of (and my participation in) the Education Crisis Team, led by Ronnie Herndon and Tony Hopson of Self Enhancement, Incorporated (SEI). We were also concerned about economic and community development. Largely due to Ronnie's negotiations with Nike, the Front successfully got an outlet store located on Martin Luther King, Jr., Boulevard. Part of the deal was for the company to hire from the community and provide employment and management-training opportunities for folks living there. Certainly police brutality and police issues were ongoing. But the education piece remained central. Our agenda focused on achieving a quality non-racist education for all children. We placed the emphasis on all children. To be sure, we spoke on behalf of African American kids, but the point we made was that deficiencies in teaching, administration, and curriculum affected all students. An absence of information about the history and culture and contributions of African Americans and other people of color shortchanged all students.

The Front's leadership shifted a bit after Rev. Jackson died. Richard Brown then came into the co-chair role. He emerged as someone who was trusted, enthusiastic, and affirmed by others in that role. He and Rev. Jackson had the same quality of being truth tellers and of following through. Their word was good. Rev. Jackson's passing was a huge, huge, huge loss. I think for many of us he was like a father figure. He had a sense of humor and a way of using stories to illustrate a point like the village *griot*, the person who carries the stories. It was a huge loss emotionally because he was always there, always there. He was such a perfect balance to Ronnie, who could be like fire. Rev. Jackson was not necessarily ice but they balanced each other very well. I think it was a huge, huge loss for Ronnie, too. The loss is still felt. I think I took his loss the way that I felt my grandmother's loss back when I was twelve years old. I can remember going to his office at the old Mt. Olivet Baptist church site on Northeast Schuyler Street, seeking his counsel. When I wanted to go work and live in Zimbabwe and I said that out loud to him, he countered with, "We need you here." He didn't say, "Don't go." He was another one who watched over me, watched me grow, and was aware of my abilities. In his own way, he always tried to affirm what I was capable of doing and to encourage what I was capable of doing. Through Mom's illnesses he was there, comforting me. I felt his loss as though a member of the family had died. And I think I felt a little lost, too, because I had a relationship with Rev. Jackson that I didn't have with my father. I looked to him in ways that I couldn't or didn't look to my dad. So I felt a void there, maybe even a little abandoned.

Additional factors reshaped the BUF around that time. Ronnie was getting death threats. The threats were really taking a toll on him (more than he was letting on) and most definitely on his family. It was a scary time. There was just not a whole lot anyone could say in public settings. We worried about the phone and probable tapping. I remember during this period being on guard about everything, publicly. We became aware of an FBI file on Ronnie. Given my experience with the Police Bureau back in the '70s, I had felt all along that the police were likely keeping some kind of file or files on us. So after Rev. Jackson passed, I remember a period of sadness as well as scrutiny, a time when we were being watched. We were wary and discerning, really discerning.

Maybe there was a part of me that just wanted to escape. I applied for another job within the American Friends Service Committee that would have involved a field placement in southern Africa. I didn't get the position. When I reviewed my application, I could see that it had not been done thoroughly. Then I realized that I was in a period of deep depression and that I really wasn't able to concentrate or function well. After a time, I was encouraged by AFSC to apply for the associate executive secretary position for the Pacific Northwest Region. I completed that application successfully and after another round of I-don't-know-how-many interviews, I was offered the job. The *Portland Observer* carried a front-page story about my appointment (I was wearing an old cast-off sweater of my sisters!). That an African American woman had emerged in that role made news nationally within AFSC. For me, it meant more travel back and forth between Portland, Seattle, Philadelphia, Washington, D.C., and New York, and more meetings focused on consensus. My meeting and deliberation skills were sharpened even more in this new role; at the same time, the organization was challenged with affirming diversity in all of its forms. People of color, gays and lesbians, immigrant and refugee folks were all finding a voice within AFSC in significant leadership roles. It was a very exciting time in the organization, one that required a lot of energy. I learned so much and it affirmed what I value about people, about working with people, and about learning from different people on this planet, as it spins with all of us together. We had better figure out how we're going to get along! That's the challenge.

At the big open house held for me at the East Burnside office, the AFSC executive committee was just blown away when they saw community people from every walk of life come through the door that day. They acknowledged: "You really do know how to do outreach down here!" The house and porch were packed out. We demonstrated through our staff work in the Portland office that we had deep and genuine ties in the community through our education program (outreach to schools, outreach to parents, outreach to young people), with the disarmament community, and with people connected with our Central America program. We would soon start a gay and lesbian program through our office. And the work focused on southern Africa continued. From a global perspective, community was coming into Portland and all of that came together under the roof that afternoon at this reception. It was amazing.

I was excited. And scared. Expectations about my leadership were on the rise again. But I was mostly excited about what I was going to be able to do with the team of people working with me in the house. So many more people in Portland, in just a couple of years, came to know the American Friends Service Committee, the Quakers, and the social justice work that we did. The work affected not only our local community but the world. But prior to my coming and the coming of a handful of others—like Karen Powell, Sherrian Haggar, and Martin Gonzales, now a Portland Public Schools board member—that hadn't been the story of the American Friends Service Committee in Portland. People wondered about this little house: "Where is it?" "What do they do there?" "American 'Fields' Service?" were typical questions. We totally changed that.

A key thing I helped to do was sharpen the AFSC's educational agenda locally so that it spoke directly to the needs of Black parents. The organization knew that parents needed help negotiating their way through the public school system and that there was a need for advocacy, parent advocacy. So if a student needed an individual educational plan, there was a need to help parents understand what that meant. Parents needed to be informed of their right to be present as well as of their need to be present in school scenarios involving their children. So we focused a lot of energy on parental rights and responsibilities and on advocacy for parents. There was some tension at AFSC about this focus. The program director, Karen Powell, and her associate, Sherrian Haggar, wanted to follow the lead of the parents. But the AFSC executive committee was more focused on systems and changing the system. We did not see this as either/or; we needed to do both. My colleagues and I believed that change was impossible without dealing with individual parental needs, getting some documented successes, and then organizing parents based on those successes. Only then would systems be not just changed but transformed. And since our program was devolved by the AFSC executive committee, there hasn't been anything like that kind of effective advocacy for parents. It was ground-breaking work.

We started with the basics. Every school is supposed have the handbook *Parent Rights and Responsibilities* and every school is supposed to make sure the handbook is available and distributed to all parents. Did all schools have them? Yes. Did all schools make them available to parents? No. If the parent knew to ask about the *Rights and Responsibilities Handbook*, they could get it but it wasn't information that was disseminated in any kind of systematic way; nor was it combined with training. Plus there was a need to focus on the different sections of information in a way that genuinely empowered parents. In addition, our program said to parents: "It's not good enough just to send the child to school. You've got to go, too." We heard about parents who had had terrible experiences themselves with schools as students; then there was an intimidation factor and the feeling that administrators and teachers were speaking a language that parents did not understand. Sometimes parents were spoken down to. So, given what we were hearing from parents, it became clear that we needed to focus on their rights and responsibilities. That's how the pilot program saw the work. We emphasized rights, but also responsibilities. Parents had to be aware that they could not simply call the Black United Front and they'd take care of it. Parents needed to engage and be accountable for the sake of their children.

That engagement meant that two staff people stretched hard to support parents, to go into schools to advocate, and then to train other parents to take on the advocacy role, as well as mobilize other organizations, like the Urban League, to step up. The model was endorsed by the community through the Black United Front. The community meetings clearly named the kind of advocacy and support needed from AFSC. I understood that if someone had a real grasp of the meaning of empowerment, then that's what empowerment looked like and that's how it sounded. And that's how it acted. But again we always had to be clear that there weren't enough resources to deal completely with the huge problem. We were doing the work that the schools should have been doing!

At the same time there were a couple of battles going on. Some were internal to AFSC. The leadership was trying to bring the organization along but many of its people were removed from the communities they served and the reality of the schools themselves. Then AFSC tried to hold schools accountable—the district, the school, a particular teacher in a particular classroom in a school, and then a particular principal. Accountability kind of rippled out. On the grassroots side of things, we took successes with individual cases or a given school and we'd come back and share that information through the Thursday meetings. People got a sense of hope and progress, and the hard work behind it all, rather than a feeling of throwing up our hands. Our message was that change is possible but everybody has to be engaged. For a time, there was energy, movement, and quality engagement around change in the schools.

The Thursday meetings were the place where progress and hope were reported. Problems were identified and problem-solving activities were also identified. That's how we knew when there were synergies to move forward. And that's also where people were asked what they wanted to do next. And that's what was so brilliant about Ronnie's and Rev. Jackson's leadership. It wasn't a leadership that imposed anything. It was thoughtful, accountable leadership that helped assess and define a situation, present options, listen for ideas, and then ask people: *What do you want to do?* And let the people decide what they wanted to do. Once people have decided, then that's where you capture your energy, your synergy.

That energy grew and eventually morphed into the Education Crisis Team effort, which included Ronnie, of course, Halim Rahsaan, of course, Tony Hopson, Richard Luccetti, who was working with Albina Head Start, parent activist Marta Guembes, and Martin Gonzalez. The "crisis" in crisis team refers to the so-called achievement gap but we redefined it to name a teaching gap, a quality of teacher training gap, and quality of principals gap. It means accountability all the way around—including for the success of poor white students—and not just resting on whether the student had had breakfast or not and wanted to learn. The BUF insisted that the Black community knew what to do in order to make change happen for students. We knew the recipe. It meant having high expectations for all students, not just some. It meant a highly skilled, culturally competent teacher in front of every student, and a highly skilled, culturally competent principal leading every school. This recipe is successfully used in a lot of other places in the country. We urged the school administration to move away from adult denial and make change happen for kids. As for those people who did not endorse change, we urged them to get out of the way. And that's where things got difficult. We believed that significant change could happen in two years. When we heard people from the schools say, "No, it can't," well, then we knew where we were. We got denial and excuse making. This has been the shameful state of affairs for decades.

Years creep by and we lose a decade. In that decade, some children wind up in the juvenile justice system. Some have gone on to the adult criminal justice system. And then another decade goes by and another whole generation repeats the cycle all over again. There was a moment in time when we were able to interrupt the damage to lives and when some things were really working better. But today they have slipped back and now there is more energy focused on maintenance of the status quo. Interestingly the language of No Child Left Behind has caused some discomfort to the status quo. Yet people were too quick to dismiss it as the wrong policy that didn't come with enough money. To me, that's the wrong conversation. No Child Left Behind meant that now we had to focus and have the conversation. And it did come with some money so how is the money that did come being spent? It has been tortuous— it has been maddening!—when I consider the lives of children lost in the mix of all the failure of adults to take responsibility for the things that they did not know how to do correctly, who were unwilling, unable to deal with the reality of their own shortcomings around cultural competency. So we keep getting caught up in this cycle of adult deficiency that is crippling the kids, and crippling kids' opportunities.

It is the shame of our nation that we have allowed this situation to go on as long as it has. I have hope in the Obama administration and the new education secretary as they frame the opportunities ahead of us. We know what to do. It is easy to see the results of our failure to invest in human potential now residing in the Oregon Youth Authority, for example, or the state adult correctional facilities, both of which I visited regularly when I was in the legislature. What many people have in common within the youth and adult systems is the inability to read. Yet while we have them within those systems, we're not focused on a systematic approach to learning to read. It's maddening, absolutely maddening. Because it's lives, peoples' lives, and lost opportunity to unleash potential and to turn lives around.

I will say this about AFSC: We had great people. We had exceptional people. We had people who were made for that particular time in Oregon. It was just that kind of team. The difficulty came with our external advisors. We had an executive committee, the American Friends Service Committee executive committee, that operated like a board, through consensus decision making. The committee was made up, for the most part, of liberal whites who wanted to do good with a handful of people of color, maybe two or three out of a couple of dozen. By and large, the committee was

removed from the reality of the communities where we were doing the work. Tension arose when we came from the community to a meeting where outsiders talked about community issues that they were personally unfamiliar with. They wanted to talk in theoretical language and often did not fully respect the experience that someone brought to the table from the community. Tension would often play out in executive committee meetings and retreats. We had a humorous way of naming this tension in our East Burnside office. A staff member would come to a meeting and say, "They're not going to have any meat. They're just going to have salad, soup, and bread. It's going to be that vegetarian fare. Remember there are some of us who like to eat meat!" And that was her way of saying that something important was literally missing from on the table. It was also a cultural thing. While we always strove towards consensus, language can be tricky. For some people language is linear, but linear thinking doesn't work for everybody. When bridging cultural divides some time needs to be invested in storytelling. Stories tell us who we are and where we are heading collectively.

The power in the executive committee lay in determining the funding and duration of programs. In terms of parent advocacy, who should decide when "enough is enough"? Are the deciders back in the community that is benefiting from the advocacy or are the deciders the folks who contribute the funds to the organization? That's where the tension was. In those meetings, two forms of truth did not stack up. One was the form of storytelling, which can be huge in terms of saving the experience for the next person who comes along and has to deal with those same people in the school or the same kind of circumstances. The other form of truth for the executive group was material that could be counted and measured. Our staff accommodated this pressure for quantification. The need to hear the stories being shared was given less weight.

Our Portland staff looked at what could be counted and measured back in the community in terms of a specific school; for example, suspensions and expulsions. We asked questions. "Is anyone collecting that information?" Answer: "No." "Should someone be collecting that information?" Answer: "Yes." "Is the school going to collect it?" Answer: "They're pushing back. They say they don't have the resources." Solution: "Well, then shouldn't we, AFSC, collect the information? And while we're at it what about disaggregating student performance and other data within school settings? Shouldn't the schools and the district be doing that?" We got push back for years and years. So AFSC and the Black United Front in the lead became the leverage by virtue of the community identifying the need for this data. At one point, we had AFSC, the Black United Front, the Urban League, the NAACP, and the Albina Ministerial Alliance all on message: We want the data. Then the demand became something else: a legislative agenda.

I went to Salem. I worked with the superintendent of public instruction, Stan Bunn, a Republican. I told him we needed disaggregated student performance data and not just from Portland but from all the school districts. He determined without a lot of push back that he could do it within existing resources. In 1991, we got our first report! That report put pressure back on the Portland Public School district and all the others as well. It was quite validating to learn when No Child Left Behind came along and required everybody to do this data collection anyway. Oregon was steps ahead because we'd already started to do it. But we started to do it because the Portland Black community said they wanted it! It would take several years more of intense legislative work to convince elected leaders of the value of having this accountability tool and reporting mechanism. Ironically, Republican leaders would take on this accountability agenda while Democrats followed the lead of the Oregon Education Association (or teachers' union) to the dismay of community activists.

In the middle of this work I realized how very deeply part of a community of activists I was. It defined a big part of my life and a good part of my time. At the same time I also struggled with bouts of deep depression. Depression would just knock me off my course and I would become unavailable. I would isolate myself. Then, as the cloud would lift, weeks, months, sometimes years later, I'd emerge, re-emerge. Under the cloud, I did as much as I could around the edges. But sometimes that was nothing. Sometimes I could only just sit, unable to concentrate enough to read. Slowly I became educated and more aware that depression is crippling and that it would be a lifelong challenge for me. I had to learn how to talk about this with family and close friends. Who could I really trust with this embarrassing part of my life?

In the meantime, inspiration was all around me. Ronnie, Rev. Jackson, and Rev. Garlington—the three of them, for different reasons—kept me going. Ronnie was a constant source of inspiration because of his commitment to people. More than commitment: He loves people. He loves Black people. He loves being of service to

Black people. But it's even beyond Black people. He has a gift for communicating hope to all people; that they, through their own actions, can make change happen. Watching him do this over and over again in different settings was wonderful. And to watch Rev. Jackson counter some of Ronnie's fire with wisdom and lessons from scripture, it was just—I keep using the word magical, but that's what it was—it was like being in a classroom. I was being taught by masters. And watching Rev. Garlington was like seeing liberation theology in action! In practice, service meant helping people discover their gifts and put their gifts to work. Edna Robertson, who for a long time was coordinator of the Northeast Neighborhood Office, also inspired me. What I love about Edna is her gift for telling stories and truth telling. I would go to her with whatever the challenge was in front of me, lay it out, and she'd come back with something from her life or with something she was dealing with. In the course of the conversation, I'd get my needs met. We both did.

Other elders cheered me just by their presence, like Mrs. Bobbi Gary. She worked with my Grandmother Randolph; I have a picture of them together in my office from the 1950s. One of the things I love about Mrs. Gary is that as long as her health allowed—she just recently passed—she would always show up for the Thursday meetings. She was one of those elders who came out to meetings that we young ones—that's what she would call us, "the young ones"—put together. We would look to Mrs. Gary for permission, literally look at her and meet her eyes in the well-used cafeteria at the King facility. "Are we doing it correctly?" "What else should we be thinking about?" "What else should we be doing?" Like Mrs. Gary, Mrs. Bobbie Nunn, who was an educator for many years within Portland Public Schools, would report to us about what was really going on. We had a number of people working within the school system—like the late Joy Hicks and Carolyn Leonard, both brilliant educators and sheroes—who would tell us what was going on in the classrooms, who would tell us what was going on within administration, who would advise us about where we needed to look and what we needed to do.

I have a funny story from a meeting at my house. I can remember saying to Ronnie: "You know, why don't you just be quiet?!" And for a moment I heard my mother's voice speaking to my father! The air went out of the room. Then the air came back in the room. It was just my way of saying to him that we've heard your opinion and it's fine but let's let some other people talk now. I return to that moment sometimes because I never asked him what he thought about it and I don't recall ever checking in with other people to ask them what they thought about it either. I was just conscious of the fact that we needed to change gears, and I successfully hit the clutch. The story speaks to the kind of trusting, respectful, and able-to-challenge relationship we had. Plus I was under my own roof.

In terms of broader relationships for our efforts, by the time I moved to the American Friends Service Committee some of the groundwork was already in place. We were able to build on that. When I say "we," I mean Karen and Sherrian in the education program. Sherrian suggested, when the Front was fighting for a middle school in the community, that it should be named for Harriet Tubman. That name was her idea and it happened. And that fact became a part of telling the story within AFSC in the executive committee and beyond. That middle school came out of the work we helped to organize in the community. The name for the school came from a member of the organization who also had the knowledge of history, sensitivity, and an understanding that Tubman was the right name for this school and for this time.

We were a group of people willing to sacrifice a lot of time and stay focused on a mission. I don't know that we saw it then as sacrifice. It was a way of life. But today I would say sacrifice in terms of what I know people gave up: time with family, health, income, and employment that included health care. Those kinds of sacrifices. My own concerns about personal safety and security went up and down. But I was always conscious. Sometimes when we did our protests and demonstrations I knew that there were going to be people present who had nothing to do with our arranged plans. I learned to be discerning and to pick people out. I developed a sense about who didn't belong and who seemed to be peripheral or out on the edges, even at meetings. There was wariness. As Ben Priestley would often say: "bears watching."

My dad expressed concern for my safety all the time. He would repeatedly ask: "Are you all right?" "Is everything going OK?" He expressed awareness about what we were doing as public activists. "Well, you know if anybody gives you any trouble," he'd say, "you just let me know. You just come to me." I knew my dad had a gun and that coming to him meant no one was going to mess with his daughter. From his own experience, he knew about what it meant to have a daughter who was active in the community and stirring things up. When A. Philip Randolph, president of the Brotherhood of Sleeping Car Porters and Maids, came to Portland in the 1940s, my dad was assigned to the security detail. He was a union member and a member of the Portland Police Auxiliary. I remember when my sister put together an exhibit celebrating African American railroad men at Union Station, I saw my dad's picture on the front page of the newspaper, up on display, standing to the side of A. Philip Randolph. Dad had his shades on and probably his gun in his pocket!

The hope and hard work of education continues. Now that I'm again able to attend monthly breakfast meetings of the African American Alliance (the Front's successor), I have my PSU students going, too. This way they can see leadership in action and actively participate as public policy issues are discussed. But the Alliance has gotten away from some of the founding practices that those of us who founded it put in place at the very beginning, when it was known as the Unity Breakfast Committee. It was founded to deal with issues but there were also traditions of community formation and affirmation, like opening and closing with prayer, that were vitally important and seem to have fallen away. There is still the singing of "Lift Every Voice and Sing"—wonderful!—but the song is the Black National Anthem, not a dirge! It's celebratory, not a funeral. We've got to work on the spirit piece. Missing, too, is space and time for everyone to introduce themselves, not just the "new" people or guests. When we don't take this time, something gets lost in the opportunity to build new relationships. I've come back physically to the meetings acutely aware that part of what I'm bringing back historically is a new "elder" role, because it's got to be done correctly if strong community is to be built and cultural traditions are to be maintained. We must be about passing the torch—intentionally passing the leadership torch to a new generation that is ready and prepared to serve.

REFERENCES
"Ron Herndon and Avel Gordly," *The Oregonian*, 6 December 1989.

CHAPTER ELEVEN

Growing and Stretching

Amazing. As many times as I have told the story of how I entered the legislature, the retelling still has me pinching myself.

In 1991, I was working at the Portland House of Umoja. I had served on the board and was asked by board members to assume the program director role. Iris Bell was the brilliant executive director and we worked together to get the program off the ground. Like our Philaldephia-based parent organization, Umoja's residential program transitioned young men coming out of the juvenile justice system back into the community and also did prevention and outreach. We also wanted to prevent young people from ever having contact with the system. I focused a lot of energy on this work, in response to concern in the community about gang activity. Some of the violence had taken lives and had people in a place of fear. We located the program in a central corner of the community, Northeast Seventeenth and Alberta, to focus on hope. We were busy on that corner. In fact, in the early days, I had an apartment right upstairs in the house. I actually lived there in order to build the program and to develop a presence in the community and in that corridor. The site had also been the former location of the Black Educational Center Bookstore. I had volunteered in that bookstore back in the 1980s, so living at Umoja was a homecoming—in a new role—to a special corner in my community.

I was also still active with the Black United Front. I took part in the offshoot organization we started, the Black Leadership Conference, which focused on a political agenda. The Conference developed a process that engaged with folks who were running for office: an interview, questionnaire, and endorsement process that was very deliberative and thoughtful. One day at Umoja, I got a call from Thalia Zepatos. I knew Thalia through our work together with the Rainbow Coalition. Thalia had also worked on Barbara Roberts's

133

successful campaign for governor in 1990. She called to let me know that she was aware that a vacancy might come up in the Oregon House of Representatives in northeast Portland and to ask me if I would be interested in looking at that position. I was dismissive. I joked about it. I was so focused on the work at Umoja it just was not a serious consideration for me.

Some weeks later, I attended a meeting of the Black Leadership Conference that took place at the Urban League, in our well-used conference room. I was seated across from Carl Talton—a friend and civic leader—who at the time worked with one of the utilities and who was also well versed in economic and community development issues and the legislative process. At one point in the conversation around the table the subject of the vacancy in the legislature came up. Carl leaned over and said to me that he thought I would be great in that role. Other people around the table piped up in agreement. And I did the old: "Not me. No, not me." I heard their words but I didn't allow myself to really go there.

I then attended a Black Women's Spiritual Retreat in Colorado. This was Women of Color as Warriors of Light, a retreat I would participate in for a number of years to come. A couple of friends from home and I went together: Adriene Cruz, my artist friend, and Guyanne Herndon, Ronnie's wife; Adriene had learned about the retreat from a friend while visiting family in New York. We traveled to Estes Park, Colorado, in the Rocky Mountains. On the first evening, which was a Thursday, the women all gathered in a circle. We were over a hundred Black women from all over the country, from every spiritual path and walk of life. And no pretense: that's why I was drawn to Warriors of Light. The retreat was about nurturing, self care, affirmation, and again, no pretense. No pretense. On this evening, after our wonderful meal together, there was sharing. Each person spoke about what had brought them. It went on for hours, into the early morning. There was rich sharing and deep listening. People revealed all kinds of things. Some didn't pay their rent or put off paying bills so they could come and be a part of this retreat. Others had special gifts that they wanted share, like massage or financial planning. So there was a rich sharing of gifts.

As I introduced myself and shared about what had brought me, I mentioned that I had received a call from the community about possibly serving in the legislature. The call was starting to get a hold of me and I shared my surprise that I was still thinking about it. Looking back, I realize that I was processing it at the same time as I was trying to run away from it. I realized, too, that as I spoke about it out loud, I gave it life. Over the course of the weekend, several women came up to me to say that they hoped that I would look at that call. They were affirming to me in their comments, as were Adriene and Guyanne. Very affirming. In Colorado, during that Estes Park retreat, I really started to look seriously at the legislature.

When I came home, I made a list of folks that I knew from different walks of life—including family and Rev. Jackson—that went to over fifty names in length. I contacted each of them to get a sense of what they thought about the possibility of my running. Across the board, people were so positive. They said things like: "Well, we've been waiting for you to do something like this." "Where do we sign up?" "Where do we send the check?" "Is the campaign committee organized?" It was so affirming and at the same time I was terrified. But it was also clear that I had support. Then a group of people came together on my behalf to help me look at the nomination and appointment process. They were all people who were truth tellers, people I could trust. Lucious Hicks IV was one of those folks; he became my campaign manager. Lucious was a past president of the NAACP and he later served on the school board. He was working with a utility company and was very much an activist in the community. He was a strategic thinker, a planner, and a thoughtful person. My sister was part of this first group, of course. So were Richard Brown, Joyce Harris, Jeanna Woolley, Geoff Sugerman, Bob Boyer, Democratic party activist; and Bea McMillan, life-long friend, served as treasurer. They helped me understand that I was responding to a call. Since I didn't wake up one morning and say, "Gosh, I think I'm going to run for the legislature!" I had to get to a place of wanting to do it. To get to that place I had to confront fear, the terror of it all. What was all that fear about?

The fear was about using my voice out loud in public; it was about being public. It involved self questioning: Did I know enough? Was I smart enough? Why me? Am I ready to do this? Am I really prepared? The support of this first group and of all the folks that I had worked with over the years really mattered in my decision. My sister's support also helped. She had worked as a legislative assistant for Margaret Carter. The knowledge that she shared about the process and how it all worked broke it down for me. That helped me get to the breakthrough place of *I can do this. I can go do this.*

So, first I campaigned for the vacancy. The Democratic Party made the decision about who they wanted to recommend to the Multnomah County Commission to fill the House vacancy (this one was created by Ron Cease's retirement). I wasn't a product of Democratic Party politics. I didn't have a precinct person's experience or party meeting attendance in my background. I didn't know any of those folks or the process. But my brilliant campaign manager, along with Bob Boyer, began to identify people from the community who could start participating in the process, become precinct people, and attend the meetings where decisions would be made. The party could recommend three to five people to the county commission, whose members then selected one from that group after a presentation and a vote. I was one of the candidates forwarded by the party. In my presentation to the commission, I emphasized how community-based activities had prepared me to work collaboratively in the legislative process, especially around human services. I received four of the five votes. The vote I didn't get was Gary Hansen's. Gary's attorney was one of the other candidates for the vacancy. Gary voted for his attorney. This scenario was my introduction to ethics in politics. Gary did not declare a conflict of interest. A few other people around me noted it but the situation was not named or dealt with. It introduced me to that other side—

the underside—of Portland and Oregon politics. It was one of those lessons that I filed away and remembered. The incident also spoke to the concern my friend Adriene raised with me about the lack of character and integrity in too many politicians.

Politics then came rushing at me. After I received the appointment, I asked newly elected Governor Barbara Roberts to perform my swearing in ceremony. Initially, she said yes. Then I heard that she changed her mind. The story was that Barbara's then husband, the late state senator Frank Roberts, intended to support Tom Novick, another sitting member of the legislature, for the District 19 House seat the next year (with redistricting coming up!). My sister told me this backstory later. Faye was a senior policy advisor to Roberts and was in the room when the discussions took place. Frank Roberts felt that Novick was Cease's true heir apparent and had kind of anointed him as "the one" who should have the seat. Roberts was also getting advice from her chief of staff, Patricia McCaig, to the effect that, if the governor swore me in, it could be seen as giving me a political advantage compared to Novick. I'm not sure how they got that; possibly there would be a photograph with the two of us that could be used in the upcoming campaign. But it was crazy.

My only thought at the time was that Barbara Roberts was the first woman governor in the state of Oregon. I was really proud about that victory; I had worked on her behalf. I would simply have enjoyed her performing the ceremony. But this whole other political thing was made out of the situation and so her initial agreement was withdrawn. Susan Graber, a member of the Oregon Supreme Court, performed the ceremony on September 30, 1991. I was honored that she said yes. Looking back, I regret that I didn't ask Judge Mercedes Deiz, the first Black woman judge elected to the bench in the history of the state, since I clearly found myself in the middle of several powerful competing dramas about race and gender in Oregon politics. Judge Deiz gave me early wise advice. "You'll do well," she said. "Do your best and don't let our people kill you!"

The next summer, the governor called the legislature into special session to consider her revenue reform package. In the preceding months, she had gone all around the state having her "Conversation with Oregonians" to help people understand that our revenue-gathering system was broken. She put everything she had—all her political and personal capital—into this effort to help Oregonians understand how state services are funded. The Democratic caucus meetings during that special session were my first. The doors to the meetings were closed. There were no media and no public in there; nobody except the members. I was taken aback by the discussion, which was so personalized. It wasn't about the substance of the package or its merits, it was all personal. The contrast with my tradition of accountability and speaking back to and with community with the Black United Front could not have been more striking. So, too, with American Friends Service Committee, where every voice and participant got a full hearing.

Those who spoke—and they were mostly male—expressed anger because they had not had enough "face time" with Roberts and had instead met with McCaig. Tom Novick was part of the caucus, so was Mike Burton. Vera Katz was there, and Margaret Carter. I looked around the room and I saw these other women. I waited to hear an affirmation of the governor's work and their championing of her, but I don't remember hearing it. What I heard instead were critical male voices and, to some degree, the female voices chiming in. I had another expectation, but this discussion was highly personalized. Some members wanted to "show her" who was in charge on the first vote. After that first procedural vote to show the governor who was really running things, then, on the second vote, the caucus would vote for the package and carry the day.

Long before we convened in special session I had decided that I would speak to the substance of the tax reform bill. This was my first time speaking on the floor of the House. I had written out my remarks and dedicated the speech to the memory of Fannie Lou Hamer. Dedicating my remarks to Fannie Lou Hamer was a way of giving myself courage to speak. In 1964, during the height of the civil rights movement, Hamer addressed the Democratic National Convention in order to have the Mississippi Freedom Democrats seated. She had used her voice courageously, urgently, and passionately in pursuit of first-class citizenship for African Americans in America. Because she had so used her voice, I could find courage to now use mine. Before I spoke, the Speaker of the House, Larry Campbell, banged the gavel to get the body's attention. Quieting the body was done whenever a new member was speaking for the very first time, but he seemed to do it with particular flair that day. It was very quiet.

I spoke in support of the governor's revenue package. I talked about why it was important as I had many times during my campaign. Then I sat down. Later—years later!—I found out from my sister that Barbara Roberts and her staff had watched the floor debate and heard me speak. After my address, Roberts said: "Whatever Avel wants from now on, she gets it." To those in the room she went on to say that she was sorry that she hadn't sworn me in. She then said some very colorful things about Tom Novick, who hadn't said a word during the whole debate. She made it very clear to those in the room that she had made a mistake. It was very pointed that I was speaking up on behalf of the plan and this other guy did not say a damn thing.

Then we voted. On the first vote, the bill failed. The second vote went thirty-one to twenty-eight not to reconsider the package. Then the package went away. All of the work went away. Democrats did that to this state. They did it to themselves. They did it to their own governor. They did that! At the time, Democrats were chided because Barbara Roberts said that people would die and then Portland Public Schools superintendent Matthew Prophet talked about all the pink slips to follow from a budget crisis. It didn't quite happen in that way but they were smart people who saw the handwriting on the wall regarding the economic future of the state of Oregon. Barbara Roberts was a forward-thinking public servant who understood that the moment called for leadership not politics. The Democrats at that time were not up to the challenge she put before them and our state has suffered every day since then from this failure of legislative leadership. Fast forward to 2009. Democrats are in charge but remain fearful of doing the right thing around revenue because they are thinking about the next election. Still. And the caucus door is still closed, so there is nobody inside to challenge how very important discussions go forward. That special session summer was definitely "State of Oregon House of Representatives 101" for me.

Election was soon in front of me, as I had only been appointed. In the primary, I faced Tom Novick and Dan Ivancie, who was the son of a former Portland mayor with some name recognition. But Novick was the golden boy. He was the one that the Democratic Party put their dollars and other resources into. Even though I got the affirmation from the precinct folks and county commission and even though they said, "We have two good candidates," the party did not think I had a chance of winning. Our campaign was grassroots. I went door to door and organized teams of folks who walked with me and on my behalf. We had house parties. I door knocked and visited with Republicans at their homes, even though conventional wisdom said that, since they cannot vote in the primary, "Why even bother?" I made the point every time I had the opportunity that if I successfully gained the vote and I went to Salem, I would represent everyone in the district. I said that early and up front. We did grassroots fundraising and concentrated on getting new people involved, registered, and ready to vote. We also concentrated on people of color and women.

The ballot counting was completed early in the morning. Lucious was down at the Board of Elections together with the dedicated—and persistent!—Geoff Sugerman, who also worked on the campaign as a strategist. We won by 156 votes, a very narrow margin. We carried the day! I was still up when I got the phone call; it was Lucious who let me know that we had prevailed. Then we faced the general election. In the general, we had the advantage of numbers, since the district was predominantly Democratic. But not taking anything for granted, I still went door to door. I even had a group called Republicans for Gordly! My Republican opponent in that race was a woman, Marilyn Schultz, a retired teacher and member of the Oregon Women's Political Caucus. During the campaign, Schultz put out a door piece that backfired. Her piece contrasted her experience with mine, making it seem like my interest was only in serving Black people. Schultz presented herself as married with children and I was "a single mother"; the names of organizations and everything else that I belonged to was "Black." It came off as blatantly racist. Liberal whites in the district were so offended that they let her know. People saw through Schultz and they went public. It became a teachable moment. Holly Pruett, a thoughtful activist and organizer, wrote a most eloquent letter rebutting Schultz's tactics. We won. And then in every race after that, there would be a token Republican candidate—I dislike the word "token"—but we prevailed in all of our races. I always made the point that, as a public servant, I represent all the people in my district. The feedback from constituents was very affirming. People appreciated knowing that the office was open to everyone, that it was the People's office.

During that first campaign, I confronted several things. One day, I knew Lucious had something on his mind. It was unspoken but I could just tell. He wanted to talk to me about my energy and his feeling that I just wasn't putting out enough at that particular time in the campaign. That exchange became the first time that I revealed to him or anyone that I was dealing with depression. It crept up. I was dealing with that, and at the same time, the other demands in my life. The depression was real. In that moment, I experienced Lucious's compassion and understanding; I also confronted a personal limitation. I didn't speak much about my depression but I became conscious that it was something that I had to more actively manage. There were times when the joy of public life would definitely be there for me in terms of meeting people and learning a lot from different peoples' life experiences. But there were also times when if felt like: "No. I can't do this. I don't want to do this. What have I gotten myself into? How do I pull the plug? Do I want to do that? Is this a 'this too shall pass' moment? Really pass?"

Another learning took place at Westminster Presbyterian Church, across the street from where I was living at the time on Northeast Sixteenth Street. My campaign team and I were working with our chart packs laying out issues and identifying people and opportunities, when Bob Boyer stood up. In his pontificating way (though I love him), he said: "Why do you want to run for this seat?" He was trying to do a role play and I just shut down. Totally shut down. Richard Brown came to my rescue and found a way with words to get Bob to back off. Richard knew—more than knew—that not only was I not ready for that kind of confrontation but I think in his mind it wasn't necessary.

Another time, Jeanna Woolley was helping me learn to talk about issues in the language of policy. That was helpful, but it was also frightening. It put me in touch with all my limitations. In my mind, I worried: "Can't these people see that I can't do this? Isn't somebody going to find that out soon?" I think there was a part of me that wanted to be rescued. Then at other times I felt: *I can do this.* I knew I could do it because I had already had the experience of sitting in the party caucus in Salem and I knew the power of voice when it's used and when it's withheld. I started to also confront what happens when you give your power over to other people or you allow other people to feel like they've got all the power. I think I ran in 1992 because it was clear to me that too many people in Salem were talking instead of listening, what I call really deep listening.

Over the years, I became pretty good at discerning when and how to use my voice. Or when to defer to others. Sometimes there are certain words that need to be spoken but not from me. But they needed to be said and so I sometimes helped other people come up with the language. In my many caucus meeting experiences, who, whether, and in what order folks will speak on the floor of the House or Senate is sometimes negotiated. Votes are also negotiated. It is possible to know, going to the floor, who is going to vote yes and no on an issue because the votes have been counted ahead of time. If members change their minds, it's a matter of integrity, protocol, and ethics to let the sponsor and caucus know, if possible. Sometimes support shifts because a member hears or learns something that changes their mind on the spot. That's just the way it happens, but it can be misread as a betrayal or sabotage.

In the midst of all the talking and the jockeying for votes in Salem I developed a reputation for being quiet. At the same time, I was always prepared to share my thinking—even if it was: "I'm still mulling this through." But I am not type A. I don't have a need to hear the sound of my own voice; it's just not one of my needs. I always check out the lay of the land. By listening carefully, I came to see that too much about the political process locks out the public. What goes on behind closed doors can become toxic. Over time I started to give voice to the view that our work in Salem should be the people's process. I began to defend the people's right to know what is being discussed in their name and how their taxpayer dollars are going to be used. That discussion belongs out in the open. What about allowing the media to attend caucus meetings? By my second House session, I started to ask those kinds of questions of myself and share them with a few, a very few others.

Most people in the legislative process do a lot of talking. I can remember any number of times sitting in a party caucus meeting with the same two or three wonderful people droning on with their Type A behavior, personality, and opinions. I was often the one to say, either "I have something to say …" or "Can we go around and hear from everybody else?" Even if people just said, "I pass," I made sure we asked and thereby insured that we had all that thinking out in the open before we marched out of the room. In any kind of meeting, it's so much more constructive to listen to what everyone has to say rather than have one or two people dominate. There is tremendous valuing in asking people what they think. What's needed is some people who are listening deeply to everything that's going on, and can find some way to open it up and then sew it all back together. It might not be sewn together in language; it might be sewn together in more understanding relationships.

What also impressed itself upon me in the legislature was nepotism and how it blocks equal employment opportunity. Oregon statutes require the state, including the legislature, to be a leader in modeling equal employment opportunity. How can we do that, I started to argue, if elected officials hire their relatives—husbands, wives, cousins, girlfriends, boyfriends—to work in the capitol? Questioning nepotism put me in a very awkward and uncomfortable place with my colleagues. And I did it publicly, in hearings and in caucus. It seemed like no matter what table I sat at with members many had their relatives working for them in Salem. I could have done the same thing. I could have hired my son or my sister. But I deliberately determined that I would not go along with that practice. How could I and then talk about the ethical "messages" that electeds send to citizens? While I understood the argument that members don't earn enough money and that hiring family members helps them make do and keep their families together I disagreed with the principle. My disagreement made it really difficult to raise the issue with Margaret Carter. We come from the same community but practice a different set of principles. She hired her daughters and other relatives. I sat in caucus, trying to make an argument against nepotism and back in the community and my district, I got a reputation for not going along just to get along, so to speak. It was very, very awkward and isolating at times.

The only time a relative of mine worked in my office she did so on a volunteer basis and only during one session. Doris Stevenson, my former sister-in-law—who will always be my sister-in-law—wanted to support me. She was retired, wanted to get out of Portland, and wanted to learn about what was going in Salem. When Senate President Peter Courtney appointed me to serve on the Public Commission on the Oregon State Legislature, I made sure the subject of nepotism came up. I was the one who made sure that it was an issue in the final report and that language identified it as a problem. Even the commission did not go as far as it could have gone in acknowledging that nepotism is a barrier to equal employment. The practice of nepotism in state government and particularly in the state legislature is not good. It is a very unhealthy thing for the state of Oregon as it has been practiced throughout state government.

I also was part of the effort to open up the party caucuses in Salem. Thank goodness that when I got to the Senate in 1996, there were allies who were ready to take on that fight. And for two sessions, we opened the caucus to light, allowing the media to sit in caucus meetings. Thanks go primarily to Rick Metsger. Ginny Burdick had a role in it as well, though she did not consider me a "real" Democrat and once even had the audacity to ask me not to talk about race, which I found shocking. It was really Rick who stood with me on the open caucus. I went to the *Statesman Journal* and *The Oregonian* reporters—even the managing editor of *The Oregonian*, Peter Bhatia, and said: "Sue us." I wanted the Oregon Newspaper Publishers Association to sue the legislative assembly. The editors said they had talked about the issue over time and that they would consider it. I raised it more than once. After the election that brought in new members to the Senate from the House, like Vicky Walker and Floyd Prozanski, those who never wanted the caucus to be open in the first place gained new support.

Caucus reform had prevailed by only two or three votes. The new members were uncomfortable with an open caucus because they thought that their words might be mischaracterized or misunderstood by the media. Other colleagues argued once again that they felt stifled and couldn't really be themselves with the media present. But in fact a lot of the personal attacks and overt strategizing for the next campaign got cleaned up with the news media in the room. And when the tide started to turn back to the closed door, I made up my mind that if the door closed, I would leave the caucus. I could not participate. I let the leadership and my constituents know my thinking. And when the caucus was closed again, I left it.

I think I had two full sessions—or maybe it was a partial session and a full session—of not participating in the caucus. To her credit, Kate Brown, while majority leader, made sure that I got information about different bills and how they were being discussed. I also went to the Republicans; or, rather, they came to me, with information. In addition each caucus published its own daily listing of bills that were on the floor with the pros and cons, from their perspectives, about the different bills. So I received the sheet from the Ds and from the Rs right there on my desk everyday. I'd look at both and I'd talk to both caucuses—members and leadership. I was invited to address the Republican Caucus to make the case for opening all legislative caucuses. And I raised the issue with House Democrats as well.

Back in chambers, when the moment came for caucus meetings off the floor, I remained sitting out there at my desk, reading, writing, meditating, or just waiting until they all came back. Sometimes folks asked: "Don't you feel like you are being left out?" I'd respond: "The folks who are being left out are the people of Oregon who don't have a clue about what's going on behind the closed doors. That's what we should be concerned about." I told *The Oregonian* and *Statesman-Journal* to take this on. It wasn't about me. It was a matter of principle. The legislative process belongs to the people.

My stance was also very freeing. It gave me back time to think. During legislative sessions things move quickly and in committee hearings too often there isn't enough time to be thoughtful and deliberative. I got time back to do some of that work. Sometimes people walked through the chamber and would observe aloud: "They're in caucus now except for Gordly; she doesn't participate." I remained on the floor on purpose to show that I was there doing the work of the people. During the first few times, I remember a feeling of uncomfortableness or feeling like "the Other" once again. Then my staff disagreed with my stance, especially my chief of staff, Sean Cruz, who argued that as one of the only people of color in the caucus (aside from Margaret Carter) my absence took a special toll on the process. I told him that I understood his point and that I'd thought that through. Carter was still there, and I was not going to go back for that reason. "Well, there are no Latino people in the caucus," he said. "No, there aren't," I acknowledged (Susan Castillo had been elevated to State Superintendent of Public Instruction). But that was another challenge and another struggle that we needed to be mindful of, talk about, and take on. It was awkward. But I took a principled position; that's where I stood. I got enough information to operate and without mistakes that would hurt my district. That was good enough for me.

During my time in the legislature, serving my district, the whole district, was my bottom line. Indeed, one of the first things I did early in my first term in the House was survey the district to find out what issues people were concerned about. We had staff support in the House Democratic office that made it possible for us to design, develop, distribute a survey. We then got it back and used the information. Used the information. What was important for me was not just collecting information but feeding it back. "This is what I heard from you. And as a result of what I heard, this is how I'll proceed. And please stay in communication." So while I had thoughts about what the key issues were, the surveys got us a

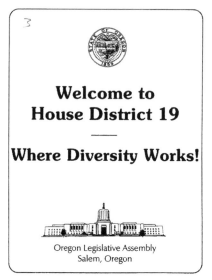

3

Welcome to
House District 19

Where Diversity Works!

Oregon Legislative Assembly
Salem, Oregon

Handbill for constituents from my House office.

reflection back. I always asked open questions that allowed people to say exactly what they were thinking. On the House side, we had a particular person, Michael Keston, who was a wonderful resource. He was very good at listening to members and then helping them put pieces together for effective communication with their districts.

Once I got to the Senate side, however, I had pretty much the same budget but twice as many people to communicate with—and fewer professional caucus staff with the same caliber of ability as Michael. One of Sean's great contributions was an e-mail listserv he developed that allowed us to communicate with people in the district and around the state. We were the first office to use the e-mail listserv in that way. We shared information with constituents about what was going on in the process in Salem. It was always important to me to demystify what's going on, explain how it's going on, list who is involved, and convey the opportunities for people to participate. And the listserv created an exchange, a way for people to communicate back to the office. We got great feedback thanking us for this tool.

Another early learning about communication on the House side came out of sitting in hearings. I recognized that someone other than me had the gavel but people from other distant places in the state came to testify; they wanted to weigh in. Yet the lobbyists usually testified first; they signed up first. They lived in Salem; why should they testify first? The people who came from great distances, like Pendleton or Medford, were, too often, an afterthought for the

148

chair. When the question "Is there anyone else who would like to testify?" came at the hearing's end, the chair would often say: "Well, we're out of time. Can you come back tomorrow?" And usually their answer was: "No." I felt that situation was crazy. I worked on a change in the House rules to require every hearing to establish who in attendance has come from one hundred miles or more. Those are now the folks who testify first. We not only identified them informally but have a form that allows the committee to make sure that people get their opportunity to be heard. It's still left up to the chair how to handle lobbyists. When I had my opportunity to chair (and even as vice-chair), I'd always move the lobbyists down, especially if the hearing was going to carry over a couple of days. "Let's hear from the people," I'd say. It would always be amazing to me that I'd even have to have that conversation!

Given my focus on process in the legislature, I developed a reputation as "the conscience of the House," and later, of the Senate. Another word used to describe my service was "principled." People also knew that I was going to spend time to do the work and that I would be well prepared. I also let it be known that our office was open first and foremost to constituents from the district. Then, constituents from other places, and then lobbyists. At that, it might be my staff, rather than me, who talked to the lobbyist. I did not like to leave hearings to meet with lobbyists. It is not good practice for our constituents to talk to empty chairs in hearing rooms. Another good example of this issue is the practice of lobbyists sending notes in to members during floor sessions. During session, lobbyists would send little notes in to have members leave the floor to talk to them. I'm sorry! I needed to pay attention to what was going on on the floor. If people wanted to see me about an issue or bill, then they needed to talk to me or my staff back in the office. I refused to run in and out. In addition to interrupting the flow of business I did not like the way it looked, as if we were doing the bidding of special interests. I didn't like it at all, so I stopped doing it early in my career.

When I got to the Senate side, a couple of members did not
know that I didn't go out. "Well, how do you put them off?" they'd
ask. I'd simply say: "You just tell them that you are not coming and
tell them to see you in your office." And they did the same thing.
There is nothing written down that says members have to go out
and meet with a lobbyist. I was also always conscious that, so many
times, young people were in the gallery. They come from all over
the state to see what we are doing and how we are doing it. And if
they looked down and saw that we're not there because we're out
in a caucus meeting, or that we're not listening as members are
carrying a bill, or that people are talking to each other in their seats,
rather than going to the side aisle, what would they think? I always
defended protocol on the floor. I remember some real low points.
A few times members would do things like shoot rubber bands at
each other and once a member started talking about lap dancing
while there were all these children in the balcony. My seat was right
in the front. I looked up at the senate president to get his eye—as
I would do sometimes—with the expression: *Are you going to do
something?!* Or I would go up and speak directly to the president.
Another way I would stop it was to ask for a "point of personal
privilege," which would not embarrass a member but would bring
the behavior to a halt.

I learned over time that there are people who treat politics—I
can't call it public service—like a game. A game. In fact, they call
it a game. And it's their personal game to go and play for a period
of time. Some members get to Salem at a very young age, in their
twenties, before they're seasoned, before they really know who
they are or really understand anything about the state and all of
its people. What they do know is that they have been drawn in to
play the game for their term. For some it is like a rite of passage. I
became very conscious that entitlement played out in the legislature,
notably white privilege. The gravity of our work on behalf of citizens
and the cumulative learning is totally missed by too many of the
young electeds and some of the staff in our state capitol.

One of my most memorable challenges to exclusion and white privilege came in my first session in the Senate. Brady Adams was senate president and we were negotiating the budget. The budget group he put together excluded representation from the city of Portland and there were no people of color and not enough women in the group. I decided to insert myself in that process and I did so in a public way. Before I did I made known to Adams what I was going to do and why: to remedy exclusion. But his public response was words to the effect that I was on "an ego trip." The *Statesman Journal* got it absolutely correct that it was about exclusion: they got it. *The Oregonian* missed an opportunity to accurately reflect the whole episode, thereby failing to inform Portlanders that one of their legislators was fighting for the city's representation on the Budget Committee. Rather than pursuing, and much less gaining, any ego satisfaction, I found the fight stressful and it took quite an emotional toll on me!

So early on in my Senate career, I got a reputation as someone who wasn't just warming a seat. My style wasn't "confrontational-confrontational" but people knew that I was going to raise principles, issues, and concerns and be fully present and prepared. And as a result of my having confronted Brady Adams, he gained respect for me and we had a good working relationship. We also had something in common. He was a bank board president in his district in Grants

This photograph was taken moments after I was sworn in as Oregon's first African American woman senator. I am applauding the gallery, where my supporters are seated. My father is pictured to the right.

Pass and I was on the Albina Community Bank board in Portland. Whenever issues related to banking would come up on the Senate floor, especially if it was something that was going to come to a vote, we would both have to declare a potential conflict of interest. My service with Albina Community Bank was a reminder to him that he was dealing with someone who was serious; just as serious as he was. At the very first meeting of the newly constituted or "unusually constituted," or constituted-other-than-what-he-had-in-mind budget group, we met in a small room. I made sure that I sat right next to him. No big deal was made about my presence, and though there was tension, the point had been made. Brady Adams was an ally on the Black community's education reform agenda and pushed the Oregon Education Report Card legislation that I supported.

Throughout my career and even going back to the early days I had very good press, in all media. So much so that other people would comment on the fact as "unusual." We didn't always get press for all the things we were doing, especially with *The Oregonian*. The *Statesman Journal*, *The Register-Guard*, *The* (Bend) *Bulletin*, and *The Daily Astorian* always did a better job of covering the legislative process. But our work was well covered and respected. Since I am someone more comfortable behind the scenes and by temperament more reserved and "in my head," it surprised me that we were taken seriously in the media. I believe it is because I held myself to high standards and reporters respected that.

It was difficult being compared to Margaret Carter in media settings and elsewhere. Difficult in the sense that I wasn't Margaret Carter. Our styles were very different. She's more outgoing and a wonderful singer. Singing is part of her ministry and she has used her voice effectively in that manner. I think we're both personable but in different ways. I don't sing. It didn't surprise me—but it surprised me—that folks in Salem expected me to sing. Of course I sang when it was time to sing happy birthday to a colleague on the floor—but this thing about singing! Some folks back in the community told me in a joking kind of way but also in a serious kind of way: "Now don't you go down there singing ..." I heard that. But

I also respect Margaret Carter for who she is. She is the first African American woman to serve in the Oregon legislative assembly and she had to invent a way of being in that setting. Her role models were white women who were trying to outdo the white men in order to be effective in their role. They had to cuss as hard as the men and "develop balls." There were old boys and these were the new old girls. That's what I observed and that's where Carter was coming from. I came to respect that but I also knew that model was not who I am. I refused to allow people to project onto me some behavior or expectation that was just not me. Once I was walking from one chamber to the other in the Capitol. I wound up in the gallery on the House side. As I was walking, a group tour came through. The guide said: "Oh, there is Senator Carter," adding, "She's the one who sings for us all the time." She was referring to me. And I said, "Oh no, no. I'm Gordly." And she said, "No, you're Carter." And I said, "No, I'm Gordly." And a third time—a third time!—she told me that I was Carter. The people on the tour had looks of disbelief on their faces. Later, I ran into one of the men who witnessed this scene, Joe Uris, who had been in Salem lobbying for higher education. He said to me: "How do you stand this? Does this happen often?" His words acknowledged the pain and shame of that moment, all-too-frequent feelings for me since so many white people in Oregon simply haven't had experiences working with Black people or even knowing any, anywhere in their lives.

153

For all our differences, Margaret Carter and I still shared experiences of exclusion and discrimination as Black women. One time, when we were members of the House, we were walking together onto the floor. It was early in a session and we were barred by one of the pages, who told us that it was "members only." We said, "Well, yeah, that would be us." I made more of a deal about it than Margaret did. I had conversations with Ramona Kennady, secretary of the House, about it. My point was that since there were pictures of all members posted in the building, the pages should know as part of their orientation and education that there are some Black people serving in the Oregon House of Representatives. Part of me can appreciate a simple mistake on the part of the pages but another part of me has endured so many slights that feel like I could write *The Book of Slights*! I could not let that episode go by me. I had to speak about it, address it, and acknowledge what it was, what it is: racism and a teachable moment.

Another time in the House, I introduced a bill on judges' tenure of service at the request of Judge Mercedes Deiz. She was still on the bench at this time. I was sitting in the front row. It was my bill. One of the members of the judiciary committee—Bob Tiernan, now chairman of the Oregon Republican Party—came in late. In front of each member's place were the bills, staff reports, and other information put before the committee. Tiernan came in, and before he sat down, he picked up the paper, quickly scanned it, and threw it in the trash. It was another one of those penetrating moments for me. I decided I couldn't let it go. I took it to the caucus and I told them that Tiernan's behavior was an affront. I let them know about Judge Deiz and explained why the gesture was an affront on several levels. Carter spoke up on my behalf. Representative Tony Federicci—who is no long living—said: "I don't live in your shoes but if you tell me that you are concerned about that, that's good enough for me." Some additional discussion was more along the lines of "what's the big deal?" But the fact that Carter spoke made a difference.

I addressed the matter on the floor. Either I did or Carter did. We made it an issue of respect. After the speech, a member of Tiernan's caucus who also sat on the committee said it didn't happen. She said she was there and it never happened. "Well, I think all of our meetings are video taped," I responded. "Do you want to pull out the video tape? Let's see the tape!" It was crazy. And it started to feel crazy. I could sense that people were feeling uncomfortable and wished the whole thing would go away—that we would just stop talking about it! But the point had been made. Tiernan did not apologize. But later I learned from him that he had traveled somewhere in Africa. He had all of these African baskets and artifacts and he wanted to share them with me. And I thought: *Good. They don't belong in your collection! Bring them to mine!* It struck me that he needed to do something to make amends, even if only indirectly. I still have the basket he gave me, and to this day, it reminds me of this story; it reminds me of who he is and who I am, and who we were in that situation. Part of me also wonders what he was doing with all those African artifacts! It was one of those experiences that was just so Oregon, so, so Oregon.

Another Oregon moment occurred when I took a concern to one of the co-chairs of the Ways and Means Committee, Eugene Timms, from Burns in rural Oregon. I wanted some information from Legislative Fiscal and needed to go through him to get it. I wound up walking with him to that office. Now, it's part of protocol in the capitol that when one member is talking to another member, as we were, staff or any other person not party to that conversation customarily waits for that conversation to end before interrupting. As Timms and I walked and talked, another conversation with someone got started around the issue that I had raised with him. Timms then asked me—no, he didn't ask me—he directed me: "You stand back there." And I thought: *What? Me step back? Where do I put this?* The words *You step back* are so loaded! It triggered for me the script of Jim Crow and so much, so much that was heavy with me for days, for days. I never spoke about this incident but it was just one of those moments received by me as *you don't belong* or *stay in your place.* Unreal, unreal, unreal.

It reminds me today of the moment in Shirley Chisholm's autobiography *Unbought and Unbossed* when she tells the story of her move to Congress from New York state legislature in 1968. She was the first African American woman elected to the U.S. House of Representatives and a congressman there used to meet her every day with words about how she got to make a certain amount of money as salary, like: "Now you get to make 42.5!" She had to finally tell him to just leave that alone and that if he couldn't come at her in a way that was civil to just not come at all. Verbal insult can create a very real climate of fear for Black women, physical fear. Once, on a tour of a transportation facility in rural Oregon, our group stopped in a

155

shop-like area. One of the workmen—I was the only the Black female in the group—looked at me and made an overt sexual gesture. I just had an out-of-body experience. What I felt was unsafe, unsafe. Feeling unsafe puts me in that trapped frame of mind stemming from all the times in my life when I have felt unsafe with no place to turn, no place to go, and no one to communicate with.

Fear—and the need to armor myself against fear and assault—permeated my life in public service. When I was going for one of my first endorsement interviews back in 1991, I had a searing experience. I was on West Burnside Street walking to the meeting, just bopping along, feeling excitement and nervousness in anticipation of the group's questioning; I was aware of facing a new kind of public scrutiny. As I'm walking along a car goes by and I hear a voice say, "Hey nigger! Where you goin'? Where you think you're goin'?" I was very conscious that it was a young voice and when the car passed me, I saw white males in the car. The words stopped me cold, in my tracks. I gathered myself to continue on my way, but I had been rocked. I felt extremely vulnerable. Would they return, I wondered, and were they armed? When I walked into the room for the interview, the group was all ready for the interview but I just couldn't get there with them. I had to tell them about what I just experienced. I can't really remember the expressions on their faces but I have shared this story numerous times and my main memory of the experience is of being assaulted on that street. I was rattled for days, for days!

My consciousness and fear is personal but much more than that; it's historical. With the election of Barack Obama, I have this stuffed fear for him. I just heard on the news that white supremacist youth have been caught plotting to kill him and their plot included killing dozens of other African Americans, named and targeted.

In my career in public service, I have experienced some moments of being at ease, of a different kind of ease. Planning the Day of Acknowledgement held in April 1999 is one that comes to mind. The Day of Acknowledgement was a series of events in the capitol designed to recognize the racism and discrimination that have been a part of the state of Oregon's history. Our ability to move forward past racism had to be about acknowledging what happened in the past. The event was led by a group called Oregon Uniting, of which I was a member, and I had a role in making that day happen. I remember sitting in planning meetings at Sunnyside Methodist Church. I put forward the idea that we should have a joint legislative session to mark that history. Some people at the meeting countered with: "They won't let us do that." My thinking has always been that the process belongs to us; it's about the people taking their proposals forward, and I remember using my voice effectively to raise up something that was controversial.

When the Day of Acknowledgement actually rolled, my feeling of ease sharply diminished. The House chamber was filled with the true diversity that exists in our state. I remember looking out into the chamber as people arrived; I saw the colorful honor guard and proud Native Americans in their formal dress and feathers. It was the first time in my experience—and in many people's experience, I was told—that the chamber looked as it did that day. My part in the program was to receive the three proclamations of the Day of Acknowledgement from the House, Senate, and Governor on behalf of the Oregon Historical Society, where a set would be deposited for posterity. As I walked up to the podium, fear came up. As usual, I had carefully prepared my remarks. I read from a letter sent to me from a woman who learned of the presence of racism in her pioneer past from family letters and how she used that knowledge to teach her children better. She had written me to say how pleased she was about the Day of Acknowledgement, because of the important message sent to young Oregonians. I intended to underscore this very point, that the Day of Acknowledgement was an opportunity to advance the work of insuring "a quality, non-racist education for all children" in the state. But I didn't say that. I said, "quality education for all children." I had my words down in my text but I held back my voice. I knew too well there were people in the room, on the House side, who had chosen not to sign the proclamation. I actually feared that my words could somehow poison the moment, that my words were redundant or unnecessary on a day already dedicated to ending racism.

I've looked back at the tape several times—and even presented the work of the Day of Acknowledgement to an international peace conference in Switzerland—and each time my choice hits me right in the heart. For weeks—to this day!—I regretted my decision to hold back the word "non-racist." I remember the faces of a couple of people in the audience, like Dr. Ethel Simon McWilliams, the renowned educator and former Executive Director of the Northwest Regional Educational Laboratory, and Ronnie Herndon. I felt like I let them down by not using the word "non-racist." I convinced myself that had they been standing there at the front of the Oregon legislature, they would have said the right word. The memory of Bill McClendon also haunted me. He always said to us young school activists: "Whenever you get in front of them and you're talking about the changes that need to happen, talk about the need for a quality non-racist education for all children, not just for Black children." I felt I'd let him down, too. Just today, however, I am writing an essay on civic engagement for the Urban League's State of Black Oregon report. I've just written the following sentence: "African American civic leaders have insisted on a non-racist quality of education for underserved and miseducated African American students—indeed for all students." In the moment in 1999, it was about the survival piece. My struggle in the legislature around language, especially naming racism, seemed to touch my very survival. Everyone has to pick and choose their words, the moment, and their arguments. But the stakes were extremely high for me as a Black woman legislator in Oregon, with its history of sharp exclusion laws and continuing threats of racial violence.

Becoming an effective state legislator involved stretching and growing, growing and stretching. It involved finding my voice and confronting fears; confronting fear on a daily basis. I had to make a friend of fear. I count fear my friend every time I'm called upon to speak publicly because fear takes me to a place of wanting to be correct. The internal tape generated from feeling trapped by fear of violation is still going in my head. And the old questions repeat: *How am I going to not fall on my face, not let people down, not let the race down?* The hard wiring is still there, even after all these years of confronting my friend Fear. Fear is my friend because, in embracing it, I get to keep stretching and growing and growing and stretching.

One of my favorite passages of growth and moving past painful emotions involved Barbara Roberts and her husband Frank. Back in the Oregon House of Representatives days I served on the Ways and Means Education Subcommittee. I was very excited about this assignment because it connected me to the work I'd done on education through the Black United Front, the Urban League, and the American Friends Service Committee. Frank Roberts was chair of the committee. One day, before the first committee meeting got started, he said, as I stopped by his chair, that he felt that I was going to be a good legislator. In that moment, I knew it was his way of bringing me into the fold. It was also a way of not quite making amends for past slights yet acknowledging "we're going to be working together. You're going to be a good legislator." I accepted his words as an affirmation. During our time on that subcommittee, we began to realize how seriously ill he was. He died in 1993.

Another day, while still a member of the House, I got word that Barbara was trying to get a hold of me. At this point she was working at the Kennedy School of Government with the program for local executives. I took her call in the phone booth at the back of the chamber. She called to invite me to be a participant in the Harvard Program. I was just rocked with excitement by this invitation. I let her know that I was definitely interested and that I wanted to do it! I loved that summer program. I loved being challenged by the rigor of the case study approach to problem solving and by the opportunity to engage with people from all over the country and the world. One day, while I was at the Kennedy School, Barbara and I were left alone together in one of the classrooms. It was after the Hon. Judge A. Leon Higginbotham, Jr., had spoken to our class—which now has extra meaning for me, since he died not too long after, in December 1998. I treasure my visit to Judge Higginbotham in his office, where he gifted me with two of his publications.

As Barbara and I talked on that day about the class, I shared words about the valuable experience of hearing Judge Higginbotham speak. Then I shared with her what Frank Roberts had let me know back in our committee days, that I was going to be this OK representative. I said I just felt called or compelled to share that with her. I think in that moment I also realized that it was a way for me to close the door on that particular piece of our shared history. She started to cry. She sobbed; she just dropped in my arms. We both had tears. It was one of those moments about the human heart; connecting in understanding and forgiveness, even if the words aren't spoken. That's what that moment was—and for me it happened in a classroom at Harvard! Like the Day of Acknowledgement—and in terms of my own personal history—a serious and honest reckoning with the past is essential to building a better life for one and all.

REFERENCES

"Tax Plan Cut Adrift," *The Oregonian*, July 2, 1991.

A Blueprint for a 21st Century Legislature, Report of the Public Commission on the Oregon State Legislature to the 74th Legislative Assembly (November 2006), p. 61.

Chisholm, Shirley. *Unbought and Unbossed*. Boston, Massachusetts: Houghton Mifflin, 1970.

State of Black Oregon (Urban League of Portland, 2009), p. 98.

Higginbotham, A. Leon, Jr. *In the Matter of Color: Race and the American Legal Process*. New York: Oxford University Press, 1980.

"Don't Forget Our People"

In May 2009, Archbishop Desmond Tutu spoke at the University of
Portland, sponsored by Ecumenical Ministries of Oregon. Bishop
Tutu spoke about racial reconciliation, and reconciliation in all of
its forms. To hear him speak and to hear him acknowledge all the
support that came from other nations in the world during the anti-
apartheid struggle, and knowing that he was talking about what
we did here in Oregon, brought the feeling of accomplishment
and connection all back home to me. He honored the fact that we
marched, we protested, and we demonstrated in solidarity with the
people of South Africa. They struggled so mightily for their freedom
and won it without a massive bloodbath. It was remarkable. As I
left the Chiles Center, I ran into several people with whom I worked
during those years. One of the women, the late Bonnie Tinker, a
Quaker long active with American Friends Service Committee, said
that of all people she had hoped that I was present because she
remembered what we had done together in that fight. We looked
at each other and there were the beams and smiles that come
when your heart is full. Our hearts were full of the moment. It was
also amazing to see Bonnie and her partner Sara Graham and their
grown children at the event; the kids were just little things back in
the day. The whole evening was an affirmation of what it means to
be a conscious human being in love with humanity and to be in the
presence of so many others who share the same belief.

It was a magical package. Everything that Bishop Tutu said made
me feel like I was caught up in his embrace. He has such a wonderful
way with language and uses humor so effectively to communicate.
Had I had the chance to personally greet him I would have thanked
him for speaking the language of hope and for his sense of humor.
Laughter is connected to hope. Even when we are enduring all kinds
of pain, it is important to laugh. I would have also told him that I

had picked up his book *African Prayers* in Washington, D.C., when I visited the African Museum at the Smithsonian in January 2008. This was a trip to participate in a National Fred Friendly Production "Minds on the Edge" Mental Health and Public Policy event. This was a highlight in my career as a champion for world class mental health treatment for all. I had made a gift of his biography, *Rabble Rouser for Peace*, to my pastor, Rev. Dr. W. G. Hardy, Jr. and to Dr. Dalton Miller-Jones, then chair of the Black Studies Department at PSU. Hearing Bishop Tutu was like things coming full circle in the South Africa chapter in my life and I listened to him and the beautiful concert that evening with a deep feeling of affirmation. Affirmation of spirit, of hope, and that all we have on this planet is one another. When it's all said and done, how we treat one another is what this world is all about. Even as we're being tested, that's what it is all about.

My work touching West Africa remains ongoing. Back in 1999, while still in the state Senate, I led a three-week trade mission for the Oregon Legislature to South Africa and Zambia, carrying a letter of introduction from Governor Kitzhaber. Dumisani Kumalo was then Mandela's head of foreign affairs. He put together all of our arrangements and meetings on the South Africa side. President Mandela was away in China but aware of our visit. From the moment we arrived in South Africa, we were treated like royal guests from Oregon. Everyone knew the Oregon anti-apartheid story! People in South Africa—everyday people, not just officials—had respect for Oregon. This respect made me painfully aware, by contrast, that people back in Oregon hadn't a clue about the stature that the state had earned in the eyes of the South African people's movement for freedom.

On this trip, I brought with me a box of buttons from all of our different campaigns from that movement. With Dumisani Kumalo in President Mandela's office, we looked at the buttons—like the one that said "Van Pelt Must Go!"—saying, "Oh, remember this event!" "And remember that event?" In the collection is a South African flag and the buttons are attached to it. Kamau Sadiki brought me the flag after he made a trip to South Africa to witness the first vote in 1994. As we moved through our visit having lunch and touring the capitol building we relived different moments in the movement that led up to freedom. At one point we stood outside President Mandela's office. Inscribed over the door in marble it says "Office of the President." I put my hand up there just to touch and feel that it was real. It was a totally amazing time.

Too many people in Oregon are unaware of the significance of South Africa's freedom and of our state's role in the movement. During my 1999 trip, Dumisani (who is currently permanent ambassador from South Africa to the United Nations) told the Oregon delegation that the doors of South Africa were open to our state for cultural exchange, tourism, and business. We had the same reception in Zambia. Only a few Oregon leaders, people like Vic Atiyeh and Mark Hatfield, people with well-developed (rather than provincial) world views, really understood what that meant. I brought that explicit message back to the Oregon Economic and Community Development Department, complete with a slide presentation from our delegation and a first-class report. To this day (to my knowledge) no one from the Economic and Community Development Department ever got on a plane to go back to South Africa or Zambia, where we had sat with the heads of government and state officials, to further develop the relationships we had cultivated.

In Zambia, our delegation met with cabinet ministers and the vice-president of the country. One of the ministers was responsible for the environment and economic development. He had studied Oregon's forestry industry backwards and forwards. They had already determined that they wanted to model the development of their forestry industry on Oregon, because of our sustainable practices. They had done the research and they knew exactly what they wanted: technology transfer. They knew that we had equipment that wasn't being used because of the downturn in the forestry industry. Their idea was that perhaps some of the equipment could be sold and be put to use. Our delegation's tour of the country included the forests and different mills. While we were sitting around that table with the Zambian ministers of state, they informed us of an international forestry conference taking place in Zambia during our visit. They wanted to introduce our delegation from Oregon because they were so honored and excited to have Oregonians present and a few of our members did attend. The Zambian minister of mines was even growing Oregon grass seed on his own land as an experiment to see if Oregon grass seed would take hold in African soil!

Such was our wonderful reception in Africa and such was the seriousness of our hosts about doing business with Oregon. Soon after our trip, the head of parliament in Zambia actually made the trip to Oregon. He met the president of our Senate at the time, Brady Adams. He met with Governor Kitzhaber. In my mind, that visit was a huge thing and Oregon treated it so badly. We were not organized or set up to take advantage of the opportunity. We did not know how. The "not knowing how" piece connects to a lack of cultural

competency on the part of state agencies and in the legislature and to an embedded fear and ignorance about Africa. What I heard in capitol committee rooms was that Africa is a land of drought, war, famine, and AIDS. Uninformed, uneducated talk. We need to learn and understand that Africa is not a millstone around humanity's neck. Africa is generous, Africa is a martyr, and Africa is the solution as has been eloquently said by Aminata Traoré.

As associate professor of Black Studies at Portland State University, I have had the opportunity to travel to Ghana as part of a delegation focused on education, cultural exchange, trade, and tourism. The Black Studies Department and PSU have a memorandum of understanding with Cape Coast University in Ghana that allows for the exchange of faculty and students. It is my hope and desire to travel back to Ghana in the next few years to help advance this agenda and a Sister City agreement between Cape Coast, Africa, and Portland, Oregon, which is being developed. My courses at PSU have focused on African American leadership, public policy, and community development. I so enjoy mentoring young people and emerging leaders who have a heart for public service. It is my hope to be a part of developing the North Star Leadership Development Institute at PSU, named for Frederick Douglass's antislavery newspaper *The North Star*, by one of my mentors, Dr. Darrell Millner. My commitment to the Institute idea brings full circle a journey of service and learning deeply inspired and shaped by Black Studies at Portland State University, which the renowned scholar-educator Millner helped found.

I am deeply grateful to Melody Rose of Portland State University and to Oregon State University Press and the thoughtful Editorial Board and staff, particularly Thomas Booth and editor Jo Alexander, for the respect and value assigned to this work and for an absolutely amazing learning experience.

In this work, too, I honor Mrs. Vivian Richardson. One day after a meeting of the African American Alliance Unity Breakfast at the Irvington Covenant assisted living center, I stopped in to visit with Mrs. Richardson. She was a resident and longtime BUF member and former secretary of that organization. We shared memories about POSAF and BUF and as we parted, she looked me directly in the eye and said: "Don't forget our people." Her words were electric and went directly to my heart. A favorite African proverb says: *When the heart is full, it comes out through the mouth.* And so it is.

A Note on Collaboration and Method

My personal connection to Avel Gordly began in Salem in the
spring of 2007. I was lobbying the Oregon Legislature on behalf
of the higher education budget as a Department of History unit
representative for the Portland State University faculty union. After
testifying before the committee, our team visited with legislators,
including Senator Gordly. She had represented my electoral district
in Portland for many years and we were acquainted socially through
my husband's political work. As it happened, a library colleague had
recently alerted me to Avel's joint gift of her personal papers to Black
Studies and the PSU library and further hinted that the staff was
shorthanded for processing it. As we wrapped up our conversation
with Avel that spring afternoon in her Senate office—she was, of
course, a great champion of our cause—I took a moment to mention
that I was available to provide support for the processing of her
papers. Her face just beamed. I had been talking with the chair of
Black Studies, Dalton Miller-Jones, for some time about collaborating
and we had not yet hit upon a project. This one seemed perfect.
Thanks to the mentoring I'd received over the years from archivist
friends, like Doug Erickson at Lewis and Clark College, I started
working on the collection, sometimes just for an hour or two per
week, during academic year 2007-2008.

In the summer of 2008, with the help of Avel's wonderful
assistant, Meggin Clay, and two college volunteer interns, we worked
full time together to finish the archive. Another key support was my
Political Science colleague and dear friend Melody Rose, who had
been leading a major effort to collect the personal papers and oral
histories of women electeds in the state of Oregon and who had
diligently laid the groundwork with PSU library to accommodate
just this kind of project. The Gordly collection is now made up of
fifty banker's boxes of materials with a detailed, hundred-plus-page

finding aid. The aid contains folder-level description for the entire collection, item-level description for half of the correspondence runs, a users' guide for teachers, and study outlines for middle school, high school, and college students. Avel already has been using material from the collection in her courses at PSU and we anticipate additional (including digital) outlets for the papers. We envision the Gordly papers as a model for community-based collection development and interactive learning. Shortly after I presented the finding aid to Avel at the end of the summer of 2008, she called me into her office in Black Studies for a meeting. After we chatted a bit, Avel looked at me with her kind and steady eyes and said: "I'm ready to tell my story. Will you help me?" I was thrilled, honored, and more than a little nervous but I said: "Yes." And I'm so glad I did.

I offered to record Avel's story to create something that I believe we called, on that very first day, an "oral memoir" of her life. My students and I had conducted oral histories in the Portland community for over a decade, but we generally stuck to "snapshot" interviews of only one or two hours in duration. In addition, those earlier projects centered on generating primary sources and archives—that is, audio recordings and typed transcriptions—for individual women leaders and their organizations rather than on generating published narratives for general readers. I conveyed to Avel that I felt prepared for but not exactly experienced with what she had in mind, but she was willing to give me a go. I distinctly remember that our conversation included some sharing about life alignments. With her retirement from Senate imminent and already teaching in Black Studies at PSU on a three-year appointment, Avel was at a good career juncture to put her story together. I shared my own sense of the fleeting and precious nature of moments that allow busy women like her to take the time to preserve, order, and share their stories. That we were both PSU faculty made arranging time together very easy. In the coming months, we often mused together about the complex histories that made us neighbors in Portland, Oregon, even though our own mothers had been born on different continents and did not speak the same language and how it was that we became faculty colleagues at a university, even though our mothers had not graduated from high school.

Avel and I recorded about twenty-two hours of interviews during academic year 2008-2009. The Gordly collection had oriented me to the spirit and scope of Avel's long career in elective office, yet I still had much to learn, since her narrative began with her childhood and family life in the 1940s and '50s. As a historian primarily of the Gilded Age and Progressive Era, I had to study up on post-1945 history and it was by working with Avel that I learned about things I should have long known, like the exact date that Dr. Martin Luther King, Jr., visited Portland, the vitality of the Black women's club movement in the Pacific Northwest, and Oregon activists' remarkable engagement with the free South Africa movement in the 1980s. Not long into our collaboration I realized that Avel's story had much to contribute to scholarly debate concerning the "long civil rights movement" in the United States and its global connections. We also became keenly aware that her narrative could and should connect with a range of audiences beyond the academy: educators, activists, aspirants to public office, Oregon electeds, readers of Avel's generation, and perhaps most urgently: students.

As we worked on her story, we envisioned a book that could work in a range of readerly settings and that contained a variety of teachable components: a good set of references, photographs (to which the narrative frequently refers), and a bibliography and index. We decided against footnotes or other annotations because they would have disrupted the flow of the narrative. We wanted to produce a volume that could fit easily in a high school classroom or a scholarly bibliography, and on a book club reading list. I believe that we have done so.

In terms of method, the two primary examples of oral memoir in my mind were Nell Irvin Painter's *The Narrative of Hosea Hudson: His Life as Negro Communist in the South* and Yevette Richardson's *Conversations with Maida Springer: A Personal History of Labor, Race, and International Relations*. These works engage with the politics of history that operate in Avel's own story. As historians,

Painter and Richardson also set high standards for transparency of method and for thoroughness. That said, their projects differ a bit from this one. Painter's work has a folkloric, anthropological dimension that is much more muted in Gordly's story. Richardson's book is a companion and follow-up to her biography of Springer. She included her own interviewer's voice in the *Conversations* volume to bring readers into the oral history process in a very direct way. I learned much from the inspiring example of these works, but ended up going in a slightly different direction.

From the first, Avel had a clear sense of the defining themes and transitions in her life, the ones that decisively shaped her choices and priorities. My phrase for how she handled these themes narratively was "juggling balls of fire." In our reflective moments, we talked about the place of repetition and circularity in human meaning making, especially in the realm of psychic or spiritual wholeness and, of course, in the context of the powerful African and African American oral traditions that she identified with. In the final version of the manuscript, we strove to retain certain elements of repetition because they pointed to how words and stories become invested with meaning over time, to the way memory works, and to the conversational quality of the narrative's eloquent truth. I'd describe our resulting narrative structure as a layered chronology—not quite juggling—especially in the middle chapters where the fireballs of Avel's personal, political, and professional life are especially hot and numerous.

After I transcribed our interviews, we had about four hundred manuscript pages. Avel reviewed these full transcripts and then I edited each down to a more conventional narrative format by removing my voice, incorporating her changes, and providing connective and clarifying sentences here and there. Avel also reviewed these edited transcripts and made a few more additions. Then she read the entire text aloud to me for final review and editing. Crucial throughout the editing process was Avel's commitment to her own story and her own voice. In the past, I have worked with narrators who, once they see their words on the page, recoil at the "sound" of their voice and start massively revising or crossing out huge chunks of material, literally backing away from their words. By contrast, Avel stood strong by her thesis concerning her particular and historic struggle with language and the authority to speak. She began the interviews with the story of her participation in the 1963 Civil Rights March in Portland, and in so doing, created an emblem that drove the structure of what became the book. As I worked the edited transcripts into book chapters, I tried to preserve as much of the oral flow and feel of the language as possible, with that historic march and its surrounding issues serving as the touchstone.

I have been greatly honored to work with Avel Gordly on this project. Now that she has her team around her—Meggin, me, her students, and our faculty allies on campus—we can look forward to supporting the many lives that her memoir and archives will have in our community and well beyond. Thank you, Avel, for trusting me with this work.

Patricia A. Schechter
Portland OR
August 2009

Bibliography

Bates, Beth Tompkins. *Pullman Porters and the Rise of Protest Politics in Black America, 1925-1945.* Chapel Hill: University of North Carolina Press, 2001.

Burrell, Raymond, III. *A History of Vancouver Avenue Baptist Church* (Portland, 2009).

Cash, Floris Loretta Barnett. *African American Women and Social Action: The Clubwomen and Volunteerism from Jim Crow to the New Deal, 1896-1936.* Westport, Connecticut: Greenwood Press, 2001.

Chisholm, Shirley. *Unbought and Unbossed.* New York: Houghton Mifflin, 1970.

Collier-Thomas, Bettye, and V. P. Franklin, eds. *Sisters in the Struggle: African American Women in the Civil Rights-Black Power Movement.* New York: New York University Press, 2001.

Douglass, Frederick. *Narrative of the Life of Frederick Douglass, an American Slave* [1845]. Cambridge, Massachusetts: Belknap Press, 1960.

Gaines, Kevin Kelly. *Uplifting the Race: Black Leadership, Politics, and Culture in the Twentieth Century.* Chapel Hill: University of North Carolina Press, 1996.

Gordon, Ann, ed. *African American Women and the Vote, 1837-1965.* Amherst: University of Massachusetts Press, 1997.

Guy-Sheftall, Beverly. "Black Women's Studies: The interface of Women's Studies and Black Studies." *Phylon* 49, no. 1 (1992): 33-41.

Harris, Duchess. Black Feminist Politics from Kennedy to Clinton. 1st ed. New York: Palgrave Macmillan, 2009.

Higginbotham, A. Leon, Jr. *In the Matter of Color: Race and the American Legal Process.* New York: Oxford University Press, 1978.

hooks, bell. *Ain't I a Woman: Black Women and Feminism.* Boston, Massachusetts: South End Press, 1981.

Johnson, Cedric. *Revolutionaries to Race Leaders: Black Power and the Making of African American Politics.* Minneapolis: University of Minnesota Press, 2007.

Johnson, Ollie A., and Karin L. Stanford, eds. *Black Political Organizations in the Post-Civil Rights Era.* New Brunswick, New Jersey: Rutgers University Press, 2002.

King, Martin Luther, Jr. *Stride Toward Freedom: The Montgomery Story.* New York: Harper, 1958.

Lee, Chana Kai. *For Freedom's Sake: The Life of Fannie Lou Hamer.* Urbana: University of Illinois Press, 1999.

Levine, Daniel. *Bayard Rustin and the Civil Rights Movement.* New Brunswick, New Jersey: Rutgers University Press, 2000.

Lorde, Audre. *Sister/Outsider: Essays and Speeches.* Trumansberg, New York: Crossing Press, 1984.

Malveaux, Julianne, and Deborah Perry. *Unfinished Business: The 10 Most Important Issues Women Face Today With New Introduction.* New York: Perigee Trade, 2003.

McLagan, Elizabeth, and Oregon Black History Project. *A Peculiar Paradise: A History of Blacks in Oregon, 1788-1940.* 1st ed. Portland: Georgian Press, 1980.

Mitchell, Margaret. *Gone with the Wind.* New York: MacMillan, 1936.

Nesbitt, Francis Njubi. *Race for Sanctions: African Americans Against Apartheid, 1946-1994.* Bloomington: Indiana University Press, 2004.

Painter, Nell Irvin. *The Narrative of Hosea Hudson, His Life as a Negro Communist in the South.* Cambridge, Massachusetts: Harvard University Press, 1979.

Richards, Yevette. *Conversations with Maida Springer: A Personal History of Labor, Race, and International Relations.* Pittsburgh, Pennsylvania: University of Pittsburgh Press, 2004.

Sanchez, Sonia. *I've Been a Woman: New and Selected Poems.* Chicago, Illinois: Third World Press, 1978.

Shaw, Stephanie J. *What a Woman Ought to Be and to Do: Black Professional Women Workers During the Jim Crow Era.* Chicago, Illinois: University of Chicago Press, 1996.

Sikora, Frank. *Until Justice Rolls Down: The Birmingham Church Bombing Case.* Tuscaloosa: University of Alabama Press, 1991. 2nd ed. Tuscaloosa: Fire Ant Books, 2005.

Smith, Petric J. *Long Time Coming: An Insider's Story of the Birmingham Church Bombing That Rocked the World.* 1st ed. Birmingham, Alabama: Crane Hill, 1994.

Springer, Kimberly, ed. *Still Lifting, Still Climbing: African American Women's Contemporary Activism.* New York: New York University Press, 1999.

Terborg-Penn, Rosalyn. *African American Women in the Struggle for the Vote, 1850-1920.* Blacks in the Diaspora. Bloomington: Indiana University Press, 1998.

Vanzant, Iyanla. *Acts of Faith: Daily Meditations for People of Color.* Fireside, 1993.

Washington, Booker T. *Up From Slavery: An Autobiography.* New York: A. L. Burt Co., 1901.

White, Deborah G. *Too Heavy a Load: Black Women in Defense of Themselves, 1894-1994.* New York: W.W. Norton, 1999.

Xing, Jun. *Seeing Color: Indigenous Peoples and Racialized Ethnic Minorities in Oregon.* Lanham, Maryland: University Press of America, 2007.

Young, Carlene. "The Struggle and Dream of Black Studies." *Journal of Negro Education* 53, no. 3 (1984): 368-78.

INDEX
Page references in *italics* refer to illustrations